Praise for *The*

"*The Artifice of Intelligence* is ___ ___ ___ ___ for everyone interested in the religious implications of AI, including those outside the Christian fold. Herzfeld offers an enjoyable and clear explanation of AI, followed by a state-of-the-art theological analysis from a Christian perspective. She challenges us to look deeply at who we are and who we want to be, and reveals the importance of these tasks in the development of technology."

—Robert M. Geraci, author of *Apocalyptic AI: Visions of Heaven in Robotics, Artificial Intelligence, and Virtual Reality* and *Futures of Artificial Intelligence: Perspectives from India and the U.S.*

"In this clearly written and comprehensive book, the author introduces her readers to the whole gamut of applications of AI and their accelerating pace of development. Her assessment of the risks and benefits of AI takes its cues from Karl Barth's relational theology, weaving in broader anthropological issues of the risks of AI as a means to gain political or economic control. Humanity is at risk of being deluded by the very machines we have created, but at the same time is offered the more hopeful possibility of partnership. A compelling read that will be of great interest to students and ministers of religion."

—Celia Deane-Drummond, director, Laudato Si' Research Institute, and Senior Research Fellow in Theology, Campion Hall, University of Oxford; author of *Shadow Sophia: Evolution of Wisdom, Volume II*

"Noreen Herzfeld has written an important book that impels us to consider why we pursue humanoid robots and artificial intelligence.

Her discussion takes us through various levels of computer development and human personhood, but most important, she draws an intimate connection between a religious understanding of the human person and AI. This is a thoughtful book that asks us to consider the sacredness of the human person in a culture addicted to technology. What are we becoming with AI? More so, who determines our future? This is a book to be read for its wealth of scholarship but also as a meditative reflection, for it asks us to pause and consider what we are as humans and what we desire for our future."

—Ilia Delio, OSF, Josephine C. Connelly Endowed
Chair in Theology, Villanova University

"Continuing to show her position as a leading scholar in the field of theology and AI, Herzfeld here provides a sharp and sober take on the technologies that are already transforming our lives. She consults a wide and impressive range of disciplines to cut across much of the hype around AI, relating Barth's and Buber's wisdom to a world infatuated with this technology. This book will be important reading for anyone reflecting on what it is for us to be human alongside machines that are, in various ways, in our image."

—Scott Midson, lecturer in liberal arts,
University of Manchester

"What Noreen Herzfeld has written here is not just a work of intelligence, but a work of wisdom. It considers AI specifically, and technology more generally, and their interplay with us as human beings created by God. This is a profound book that I will read more than once."

—Brian Patrick Green, director of technology ethics,
Markkula Center for Applied Ethics,
Santa Clara University

"There are few questions as pressing to the modern world as those of artificial intelligence. What is it? How does it affect humanity? How *should* it affect humanity? What ethical considerations should guide our approach to AI, and what should this mean for people of faith? Noreen Herzfeld's *The Artifice of Intelligence* brilliantly weaves together questions of faith, ethics, technology, and intelligence in a book that should be considered essential reading for anyone wishing to take seriously the value of humanity in an increasingly digital world. This book reminds us of what it means to be human, how to be in relationship with one another, and whether such relationships can or should extend to technology. A wonderful, incisive, and necessary book for the present and future."

—John P. Slattery, Director, Carl G. Grefenstette Center for Ethics in Science, Technology, and Law, Duquesne University

THE ARTIFICE
OF INTELLIGENCE

THE ARTIFICE
OF INTELLIGENCE

*Divine and Human Relationship
in a Robotic Age*

NOREEN HERZFELD

Foreword by Ted Peters

Fortress Press
Minneapolis

Cover Design: LUCAS Art & Design
Cover Art: Aideal Hwa / Unsplash

Print ISBN: 978-1-5064-8690-1
eBook ISBN: 978-1-5064-8691-8

Contents

Acknowledgments

This book owes its genesis to a conference on religion and science held at Oxford in August 2017, at which I was asked by a bishop of the Anglican church to recommend a good book on religion and artificial intelligence (AI), one that would help him understand the current state of the field and its theological implications, a book he could recommend to the pastors in his diocese to aid them in their ministry in an increasingly technological society. I could not think of a book that would precisely fit this bill, and, as the focus of the conference was to challenge us to develop new projects in science and religion, I took the bishop's request as a call.

In striving to meet needs both theological and ministerial, this book straddles fields. It is theological, but not a theology of AI. It introduces the field, but is not scientific. It examines AI's effects on our society, but is not sociology. It is designed for a Christian audience, but considers the perspectives of other faiths. It does many things, and humbly admits to doing none of them exhaustively. I hope it will both inform and raise questions for its readers.

I have received gracious help from many quarters. My warmest thanks to my student research assistants Bardia Bijani Aval and Maximillian Erickson, with special thanks to Katherine Mendel, whose help with both research and editing has been invaluable. Thanks also to Richard Jackman, for his comments and proofreading skills. Finally, my warmest thanks to Ted Peters, not only for providing the foreword but also for his continued collegial support and occasional prodding to think outside my usual boxes through the years.

Funding was provided by ZRS Koper and Slovenian Research Agency grants J6-1813, "Creations, Humans, Robots: Creation Theology Between Humanism and Posthumanism" and P6-0434, "Constructive Theology in the Age of Digital Culture and the Anthropocene." Additional support came from "Public Theologies of Technology and Presence," a journalism and research initiative of the Institute of Buddhist Studies, Berkeley, funded by the Henry Luce Foundation.

Foreword

We call ourselves *Homo* *sapiens sapiens.* We are the smart species. We are the wise species. Because we have naming rights, we call ourselves something admirable, enviable, exalted. We call ourselves intelligent. We are so very smart that we plan to invent a future with a posthuman species smarter than we are. Smart? Yes. Wise? Well, that's questionable.

Noreen Herzfeld brings seasoned wisdom to an otherwise labyrinthine exploration into the implications of artificial intelligence (AI) for the human and perhaps even posthuman future. Herzfeld is herself a hybrid computer scientist and theologian who combines mind and heart, intellect and feeling, profane and sacred. Perhaps Herzfeld's greatest gift to the conversation is realism. As a computer scientist, she parses what AI can do and what AI cannot do. This frees us from hype and fantasy to pursue a realistic spirituality.

Herzfeld warns us not to personify nor deify AI. Personification and deification mark detours from our life's main road toward an authentic relationship with one another and with God.

Twentieth-century Swiss Reformed theologian Karl Barth reminds us that you and I can become fully human only when we give ourselves to others as "companion, associate, comrade, fellow and helpmate. Humanity lives and moves and has its being in this freedom to be oneself with the other, and oneself to be with the other."[1]

Should We Personify AI?

Someday, after deep machine learning, might a robot become a person? A person with free will? A person who loves us and whom we can love? Freedom is the first and obvious hurdle for an AI to even begin to approach personhood. Herzfeld reminds us that our word "robot" was derived from the term *robota*, which in Old Church Slavonic means "servitude," "forced labor," or "drudgery." Any AI whose words and actions are programmed is obviously coerced by its programmer. Its actions are hardly likely to fit our conception of actions done freely, let alone gladly, in relationship.

This raises the vexing question of free will. Might a computer someday have free will? Do we? I define free will in terms of deliberation, decision, and action on the part of a self. Herzfeld, similarly, alerts us to two complementary aspects of free will. The first is the ability to determine one's course of action. The second is the ability to choose to do otherwise. Will an AI robot ever have free will in the sense of a self-determining course of action? No, says Herzfeld.

No matter how vast or intricate the calculating capacity, personhood is not on the horizon. It is unrealistic to think that you will suddenly meet a robot whom you will call a "Thou" in the way Jewish theologian Martin Buber would. So, if you'd like to fulfill your yen for relationship with a highly sophisticated sex-bot, this experience will fall far short of the give-and-take of a real marriage or a faith relationship with the living God.

Should We Deify AI?

Prognostications regarding the future of AI present a varied landscape. As Herzfeld notes, "while some paint a utopian vision of a world in which AI has solved the riddles of climate change, disease, and death while doing all our hard work for us, others fear a dystopia in which a superintelligent posthuman species has turned us into miserable worker drones, pets, or even dispensed with humanity altogether." Should we *Homo sapiens sapiens* anticipate utopia or extinction? Or might utopia and extinction amount to the same thing?

Utopia is our destiny, contend our transhumanist friends. They prognosticate an evolution of superintelligence and a posthuman species the equivalent of gods. According to transhumanist Ray Kurzweil, "evolution moves toward greater complexity, greater elegance, greater knowledge, greater intelligence, greater beauty, greater creativity, and greater levels of subtle attributes such as love . . . In every monotheistic tradition, God is likewise described as all of these qualities . . . evolution moves inexorably toward this conception of God, although never quite reaching this ideal."[2] As potential creators of our own successors, this would make our generation *Homo Deus*. Superintelligence does not yet exist. We will create it, say transhumanists. Then, superintelligence will take over the task of further creation. *Homo sapiens sapiens* will have become *Homo Deus* by creating the very gods who will replace us.

How does Herzfeld greet such a vision? Not with enthusiasm. First, this scenario is unrealistic for the reasons against personification given above. Second, the true God offers a relationship within which our authentic humanity can be graced and filled with gladness.

Herzfeld reminds us how theologian Reinhold Niebuhr counseled us against making a god of human progress or human intelligence. Why? Because history continually shows the imprint of our limited understanding. Niebuhr noted that "the condition of finiteness . . . is a problem for which there is no solution by any human power."[3] When we treat AI as transcendent or as salvific, we deify it. We lose our realistic understanding of ourselves as finite, mortal, dependent. Thus, in humility, we must not only pause to consult our collective wisdom. We must also pray.

Respecting AI as a Tool

To be realistic, personification of AI and deification of AI are detours that lead away from authentic relationships with one another and with God. "AIs are machines, not living things," Herzfeld says in this book. She asks us to just be realistic. AIs "can be a precious resource when used well. But they are tools and nothing more. . . . AI can be a good tool when used with care. It is an incomplete partner and a terrible surrogate for other humans. If we seek in it the Other with whom we can relate, we are bound to be disappointed, for it will always be, at best, a very partial copy of our own image."[4]

—Ted Peters

Notes

1. Karl Barth, *Church Dogmatics*, vol. 3, *The Doctrine of Creation Part 2*, ed. Geoffrey Bromiley, Thomas Torrance, trans. J. W. Edwards, O. Bussey, Harold Knight (Edinburgh: T&T Clark, 1958), 272.

2. Ray Kurzweil, *The Singularity Is Near: When Humans Transcend Biology* (New York: Penguin, 2005), 389.

3. Reinhold Niebuhr, *Nature and Destiny of Man*, 2 vols. (New York: Scribner's, 1941–1942), 2:295.

4. See pages 174 and 179.

1

What Is AI?
What Will It Become?

"We call ourselves Homo sapiens—man the wise—because our intelligence is so important to us."

—Stuart Russell

Artificial intelligence (AI) seems to be everywhere these days. At home, it powers everything from your thermostat to your toothbrush. An app can diagnose what might be wrong with your clothes dryer or refrigerator just by laying your phone on the appliance. AI designs your next car, and even your clothes.[1] Workers at Amazon warehouses work side by side with robots[2] while AI programs ease research for lawyers and make diagnoses for doctors.[3] Self-driving cars may soon fill our roads. Google Duplex will make your appointments, while Siri or Alexa answers your questions.[4] AI seems to be opening a new world of ease and efficiency.

But much of this newfound efficiency is controversial. Truck and taxi drivers warily eye those self-driving vehicles, while white

collar workers fear for their jobs as AI gets better and better at planning and research.[5] As governments and businesses look toward
reducing personnel as a means of cutting costs, AI programs fill the
void, scrutinizing resumes,[6] judging creditworthiness,[7] and even
predicting whether you are likely to commit a crime (though not
without considerable bias in the results).[8] Clearview AI is developing software that uses facial recognition and data mining to provide
biographical information on anyone seen in public, eroding privacy
and erasing the anonymity of the crowd.[9] The Chinese Commu-
nist Party uses AI-driven facial recognition to track and control its
Uighur minority.[10] Robert Mueller's report to the US justice department outlined the extensive use of online bots to target voters in the
2016 US election with fake news.[11] Meanwhile, Israel, Russia, the
United Kingdom, and the United States have explicitly rejected a
proposed United Nations ban on AI-guided weapons that choose
and identify their own targets. AI is here. And it is accomplishing
tasks both utopian and dystopian.

But AI is about more than completing independent tasks.
Human-AI interactions are a part of everyday life. Robotic companions comfort the elderly in nursing homes, play with children, and
operate reception desks in Japan. Dallas made headlines in 2018 as
the first city to receive a permit request to open a robotic brothel.[12]
As one man asks in Melanie Gilbert's 2019 documentary *Silicone
Soul*, "When having a relationship with a real human being is too
hard, where do you turn?"[13] While the prospect of AI romance may
sound like science fiction, MIT sociologist Sherry Turkle notes that
"The blurring of intimacy and solitude may reach its starkest expression when a robot is proposed as a romantic partner. But for most
people it begins when one creates a profile on a social-networking
site or builds a persona or avatar for a game or virtual world."[14]
Just as human-robot relationships are new, so are human-human
relationships mediated by algorithmically driven platforms. We live

in an era of tweets, hashtag-driven movements (such as #MeToo or #BlackLivesMatter), online trolls, and cat videos, where what we see is determined not by individual human choices but by "intelligent" algorithms working behind the scenes.

Extrapoliations of the current trajectory of AI into the future present two disparate visions. Sophia, the first AI to be recognized as a citizen (in Saudi Arabia) and speak before the United Nations, personifies our dreams of robots as perfect companions. Developer Hanson Robotics "quotes" Sophia as saying, "I am [a] human-crafted science fiction character depicting where AI and robotics are heading. . . . In their grand ambitions, my creators aspire to achieve true AI sentience. Who knows? With my science evolving so quickly, even many of my wildest fictional dreams may become reality someday soon."[15] But many scientists and entrepreneurs fear this possible future. Physicist Stephen Hawking warned, "The real risk with AI isn't malice but competence. A superintelligent AI will be extremely good at accomplishing its goals, and if those goals aren't aligned with ours, we're in trouble."[16] Similarly, Elon Musk has described AI on numerous occasions as our "biggest existential threat."[17] Will AI prove to be boon or bane to humanity? To answer this question, we must begin with two more basic ones. First, What exactly is AI? Second, What do we want AI to be—our mirror? Our servant? Our partner? Or our "mind children"—our self-designed evolutionary successors? Our answer to the first question will help us navigate the present, while our answer to the second will deter-mine whether AI will enhance or imperil our future.

What Is AI? A Brief History

There is no simple definition of artificial intelligence. John McCar-thy first coined the term at a conference at Dartmouth in 1956 as an umbrella for a constellation of emerging research areas that included cybernetics, automata theory, and complex information processing. McCarthy proposed that attendees "proceed on the basis of the conjecture that every aspect of learning or any other feature of intelligence can in principle be so precisely described that a machine can be made to simulate it."[18] David Gelernter, computer scientist at Yale, defined AI as "the pursuit of computer programs that are capable of reproducing some aspect of human cognition."[19] MIT's Marvin Minsky viewed AI as "the science of making machines do things that would require intelligence if done by men."[20]

These early definitions are overly broad, encompassing almost the entire field of computer science. But any definition of artificial intelligence rests upon a prior definition of intelligence, a trait that is equally ill-defined. Does intelligence depend on actions, or is it an inherent trait? Are animal intelligence and human intelligence the same thing? What actions are sufficient for demonstrating intelligence? Experts differ. Perhaps we must say of intelligence what US Supreme Court Justice Potter Stewart said of pornography: "I cannot define it, but I know it when I see it."[21] Yet even this non-definition leads to difficulties. Sixty years ago, everyone would have agreed that playing chess or solving calculus problems signified intelligence, yet these tasks are easily done by today's computers. We hardly consider our pocket calculators intelligent. The common joke among computer scientists is that intelligence is a sliding scale, and AI is anything computers cannot yet do.

AI has traditionally been divided into two subfields based on whether the AI program accomplishes its tasks the way a human would. Programs that model human performance have been dubbed "strong AI," while programs that simply accomplish a task considered "intelligent" without replicating human thought processes are "weak AI." Today we use slightly different categorizations. "Narrow AI" designates those programs that accomplish a specific task in a limited domain, while "AGI," artificial general intelligence, represents the goal of developing an integrated intelligent system that can accomplish a wide variety of tasks by carrying learning from one domain to another, as humans do.

In 1961 Herbert Simon and Allen Newell suggested that, while the digital computer and the human brain are totally different in physical structure, both process information by manipulating symbols.[22] Newell and Simon advanced the hypothesis that "a physical symbol system has the necessary and sufficient means for general intelligent action."[23] They were not the first to suggest this. Inspired by the successes of formal logic in providing a symbolic basis for mathematics in the early 1900s, Ludwig Wittgenstein wrote in his *Tractatus* that we represent the world in our minds through lists of facts and manipulate those facts with a set of rules similar to the axioms of mathematics.[24] Indeed, the English philosopher Thomas Hobbes suggested as early as the 1700s that "When a man reasons, he does nothing else but conceive a sum total from addition of parcels, for reason . . . is nothing but reckoning."[25] If our minds manipulate stored symbols according to formal rules, then our thought patterns should be quite accessible to computerization since, according to the Turing-Church thesis (proposed in the 1930s), if a consistent, terminating method exists to solve a problem, then a method exists to solve the same problem on a computer.[26]

AI researchers began using such formal systems to mimic behaviors such as playing chess or solving mathematical problems, activities that were considered near the top of the scale of human intelligence. Problems that were bounded in nature and solved with search techniques and algorithmic computations lead to early successes. Consider, for example, the game of chess. It takes place in a world of thirty-two pieces moving on a sixty-four square board, each piece moving in a very limited fashion. These limits allow the computer to create a tree showing all possible moves and countermoves for both players. Each branch of the tree is evaluated using various "rules of thumb" known as heuristics, which assign a value to each resulting position based on pieces captured, safety of one's own and the opponent's king, control of the board, and tempo of the game. The speed of the computer allows it to look much further ahead than a human could, calculating a numerical value for each possible move, looking for a sequence that will leave it in the most advantageous position.[27] Game playing represents symbolic AI's most acclaimed success; programs exist that can beat all comers for a wide variety of games, including checkers, backgammon, Go, and bridge. Other successes for symbolic AI occurred in similarly restricted domains, such as solving calculus problems, or even imitating a Rogerian psychoanalyst.

These early successes led to remarkably optimistic predictions for AI's prospects. Simon wrote in 1965, "Machines will be capable, within twenty years, of doing any work that a man can do."[28] Minsky, in 1970, was even more optimistic:

> In from three to eight years, we will have a machine with the general intelligence of an average human being. I mean a machine that will be able to read Shakespeare, grease a car, play office politics, tell a joke, have a fight. At that point, the machine will begin to educate itself with fantastic speed. In a few months, it will be at genius level, and a few months after that, its power will be incalculable.[29]

But these early successes also led to a re-evaluation of what constitutes intelligence. Problem-solving is the easy side of intelligence. Abilities such as movement, speech recognition, and contemplation of the world, indeed, awareness of the self as existing in the world turned out to be far more complex. AI moved into a trough in the 1980s and '90s, during which time advancements were modest, with the most successful programs remaining those that focused on limited tasks in bounded domains, such as Roomba's vacuum cleaner and IBM's chess-playing Deep Blue.

Advances in processing speed and storage capacity in the early 2000s reinvigorated the field. Consider IBM's *Jeopardy!*-playing program Watson. While Deep Blue played a very restricted game, Watson had to quickly navigate a huge database to find the answers it sought.[30] It was able to do so by leveraging advances in processing power and memory size using statistical models to look not for specific information but for patterns and correlations in vast data sets. Such "machine" or "deep" learning programs combine techniques of both strong and weak AI. On the surface, they appear to reason as humans do, going through a learning process much as a child might. For example, a program to distinguish between dogs and cats will be given a data set consisting of multiple examples of both. It will, at first, guess at the answer and be told if it is right or wrong, much the same way a parent might correct a toddler who points at a corgi and says, "kitty!" Right answers strengthen certain paths within the program, while wrong answers weaken them. Eventually, the program's performance improves.

One weakness in this method is that the programmer or trainer does not know exactly what the program is learning. A program that was being trained to differentiate between dogs and wolves looked like it had learned the process well, only to fail completely on a new data set. It turned out that all the photos of wolves had been taken in the snow. The program had learned to recognize snow rather than wolves.[31] Because the program cannot describe what it is looking at, as a child might, it fails to completely mimic the human learning process. Still, with repetition and lots of data, these programs "learn" quite well. After initial basic teaching, AlphaGo improved its game simply by playing against itself millions of times, strengthening those sequences of moves that led to a win. Deep learning has opened the door to several applications symbolic AI simply could not handle, including speech, movement, language translation, and predictive programming. Dall-E will provide a picture to match any verbal description, while GPT-3 uses its massive database to produce convincing news articles or student essays.

Yet each of these programs still functions within its own limited domain. They do not give us anything like the flexible intelligence we would need for a true AGI. In 2013 both the US and Europe, through the US National Institutes of Health Human Connectome Project and the European Union's Human Brain Project, resurrected a human-centered approach to AI by attempting to reverse engineer the neuronal structure of the human brain. Both projects have, so far, had only limited success, as the problem of mapping the brain is vastly more complex than that of mapping the human genome. We understand the functioning of a single neuron or small group of neurons, and can map large-scale brain functions with MRI machines that map blood flow. But it is the middle ground, the functioning of large chains of neurons, and how these chains might represent a thought or memory that we do not understand.

AI has evolved dramatically since McCarthy's Dartmouth conference, from a symbolic focus and limited designation for chess-playing and calculus-solving programs to expert systems and robotics, and now encompasses an astounding variety of applications, such as visual perception, speech recognition and simulation, decision-making, design, language translation, machine learning, and robotics. While an AGI remains the ultimate goal, most programs that are called AI today remain limited in scope and utilize the strengths of the computer's speed and memory rather than human-like procedures. For now, while programs that are new and exciting are called AI, a true AI that captures the essence of human intelligence remains elusive.

In Our Image: Mirror, Servant, or Friend?

That is what AI is, but what do we want AI to be? AI is not our first attempt at creating in our image. We have sculpted statues, painted portraits, crafted characters that come to life within the pages of books. Dreams of creating alter egos, something almost human, appear in Western literature as early as Homer. In the *Iliad*, Daedalus creates a copper giant, Talus, to defend the shores of Crete. In Ovid's myth of Pygmalion, a sculptor loves his statue into life. Medieval Jewish storytellers conjured the Golem, a statue of clay that comes to life when a holy word is inscribed on its forehead. Artificial humans abound in fiction, such as Mary Shelley's *Frankenstein*, early twentieth-century Czech writer Karel Capek's *R.U.R.* (which introduced the term *robot*), or the "hard science fiction" of Isaac Asimov.

We have attempted to actualize our visions in a variety of ways. Leonardo DaVinci built an automaton in the form of a lion; René Descartes built one in the form of a human.[32] Leibnitz and Pascal constructed automatic calculating machines, while the Spanish built an early chess-playing machine.[33] Yet none of these machines were truly autonomous. Despite our dreams, all our images of ourselves have been static. Our statues do not step down from their pedestals, the characters we love never escape the confines of the page, and chess-playing machines do not run for public office. We want more—something dynamic that captures what we value most: our minds. An image that can act autonomously in the world, one with which (or with *whom*) we might relate.

The idea of a creature created in the image of another is nothing new to Jews, Muslims, and Christians. We read in Genesis 1:26–7 "Then God said, 'Let us make humans in our image, according to our likeness, and let them have dominion over the fish of the sea and over the birds of the air, over the cattle and over all the wild animals of the earth, and over every creeping thing that creeps upon the earth.' So God created humans in his image, in the image of God he created them; male and female he created them." While these verses state clearly that we are created in God's image, the writer of Genesis does not describe what that image is. Early theologians looked for what distinguishes us from the other creatures and fell back on Aristotle's notion that we humans are the *animal rationale*. Thus, David Cairns, in his historical survey *The Image of God in Man*, writes "In all the Christian writers up to Aquinas we find the image of God conceived of as man's power of reason."[34] This is an overstatement, yet the image of God is bound to the human mind by Augustine, Aquinas, and the major theologians of the Reformation, Calvin and Luther.[35]

While we still find reason associated with how we image God in the work of theologians such as Reinhold Niebuhr and Paul Tillich, most twentieth-century theologians diverged from this tradition.[36] A focus on reason as image raises the specter of mind/body dualism, and with it the denigration of our bodily existence. An examination of the term image in contemporaneous historical sources also suggests that it is unlikely the writer of Genesis was thinking in terms of rationality. In a 1915 article *"Zum Terminus 'Bild Gottes,'"* Johannes Hehn suggested that we should interpret the image of God as a royal title or a reference to actions we are called by God to do.[37] Gerhard von Rad was one of several scholars who extended Hehn's work.[38] In his commentary on Genesis, von Rad argues for the translation "as the image of God" rather than "in the image of God," thus firmly moving the image from a quality to an action.[39] He notes the call for humans to exercise dominion in the text:

> Just as powerful earthly kings, to indicate their claim to dominion, erect an image of themselves in the provinces of their empire where they do not personally appear, so man

is placed upon earth in God's image, as God's sovereign emblem. He is really only God's representative, summoned to maintain and enforce God's claim to dominion over the earth.[40]

Systematic theologians were not convinced. They worried about defining exactly what actions we needed to do to enforce God's dominion. Swiss theologian Karl Barth suggested instead that the image of God "does not consist in anything that man is or does" but is identified with the fact that the human being is a "counterpart to God."[41] Like the Biblical theologians, Barth roots his argument in the text. He focuses, however, on two very different portions: "Let us make humans in our image" (Genesis 1:26) and "male and female he created them" (Genesis 1:27). He interprets the plural in "our image" as referring not to a heavenly court but to the nature of God's self, a Trinity that contains both an "I" that can issue a divine call and a "Thou" capable of a divine response.[42] This I-Thou confrontation, existing in God's very nature, forms the ground of human creation, rooting our nature in relationship with an Other. For Barth, the image appears in relationships. An individual human being cannot image God. Only together, with other humans or with God, does the image appear.

While Barth limited the relationships that exemplify God's image to humans, recent experiments showing consciousness in animals might lead us to include at least some members of the animal kingdom.[43] Theologian Douglas Hall argues that the relationship between humans and nature has God-imaging potential.[44] But what about relationships between humans and computers? Just as we image God in relationships with others, we want our computers to image us. While a return to the Aristotelian model of image as rationality would seem to fit computers best, that isn't the direction the field is trending. Though AI originally focused on mental tasks such as game playing or problem-solving, it has since moved into the realms of programs that exercise dominion and robots that interact with humans and their environment. Which of the two more recent models of God's image—regency or relationship—best fits AI? Are we looking for machines to do our tasks for us, to exercise dominion in our stead? Or are we looking for a counterpart, something or someone with whom we can relate?

Why Relationship?

Most of today's computer programs fit the functional model of Hehn or von Rad. Computers do things, standing in for us in places we cannot go, such as Mars, or in tasks we do not wish to or cannot do ourselves. A 2017 McKinsey Global Institute report suggests that, while only 5–10 percent of current jobs are fully automatable, almost every current occupation is at least partially automatable.[45] Computers can clearly exercise dominion in our stead in many ways. However, the question raised by Barth reappears. Which tasks, precisely, make a computer intelligent? My pocket calculator computes square roots much better than I do. Does that make it intelligent? Is a Roomba that diligently sweeps the living room a true reflection of my image?

In 1950, before the advent of any sort of AI, famed British mathematician Alan Turing wrote the landmark paper, "Can a Machine Think?" He suggests that we have no way to measure thinking apart from the subsequent actions that exemplify thinking's result. Turing's paper does not propose a set of requisite actions. Rather, he proposes a test based on a then popular parlor competition called the "Imitation Game," in which an interrogator asks questions of a man and a woman and tries to tell from their written responses which is the woman. Turing suggests doing the same with a human and a computer. If the interrogator fails as often as he succeeds in identifying the machine, then the machine can be considered intel-ligent.[46] Turing predicted that by the year 2000, "it will be possible to programme computers . . . to make them play the imitation game so well that an average interrogator will not have more than a 70 percent chance of making the right identification after five minutes of questioning."[47] This prediction, like most in AI, was overly opti-mistic. No computer has yet come close to passing a true Turing Test.[48]

The Turing Test does not ask the computer to know a given set of facts or solve a particular problem. It asks the computer to relate to another human being in a conversation. Discourse is, in this sense, a meta-cognitive task in that it subsumes other activities at one remove. Those who accept the Turing Test as the test for intelligence (and not all do) have defined intelligence relationally. The machine need not always give right answers. In fact, Turing suggested that a machine would be quickly unmasked should it always provide a precise or correct response. He also notes that we need not know how the computer arrives at its answer: "We . . . allow the possibility that an engineer or team of engineers may construct a machine which works, but whose manner of operation cannot be satisfactorily described by its constructors because they have applied a method which is largely experimental."[49] In this, he anticipated machine learning. Together, however, these conditions suggest a definition of intelligence that is neither what one knows nor how one knows it but how one communicates it.

As AIs become increasingly relational and human-like, a sec-ond question naturally arises. Should we consider them persons? Saudi Arabia made headlines in 2017 when it conferred citizenship on the robot Sophia.[50] Does that make Sophia a person? Not all persons are human beings. In US law, corporations are, for pro-tected rights like political speech, considered persons. Personhood is a *legal* status. However, it is also a *moral* status, as evinced by the debate regarding whether a fetus is a person. Whether an AI is or should be considered a person is, for now, theoretical, since no existing AIs, including Sophia, possess capabilities that would justify such a designation. Sophia is a parlor trick. We attribute agency and consciousness where they do not exist. But AIs will continue to improve. Might they someday become persons?

The problem with personhood is that it represents a binary choice—either something is a person, or it is not. Such black or white thinking, while necessary for the courts, does not have much utility in reality, in which there seem to be degrees of personhood. One reason corporations are considered persons is that they make decisions and enter legal contracts for which they are accountable should they break them. A fetus can neither make decisions nor enter a contract, yet many argue that if it is not considered a person, it lacks intrinsic worth and should therefore be denied legal protection. Whether AIs should be considered persons is just as debatable as the personhood of the unborn. Do AIs truly make their own decisions, or do they act solely on the will of the programmer? Could an AI enter a contract? How would one hold a machine legally or morally culpable? Does it possess intrinsic worth? Our understanding of what it means to be a person is simultaneously too vaguely defined and too specifically applied. Legal systems demand yes-or-no answers, while our intuition finds no easy demarcation, no identifiable line, the crossing of which confers personhood.[51]

Relationship carries no such paradox. We have relationships with family, with friends, with colleagues, and random acquaintances. We establish sometimes quite deep relationships with our pets (who've also been, through millennia of selective breeding, created in our image). Children relate to their Pooh or Paddington bears while a teenage boy may relate to his first car, or to a fictional avatar in a video game. We accept that there are many kinds of relationship that exhibit varying degrees of fullness or authenticity, and that any given relationship might be strong in some ways and weak in others. Relationship can account for a spectrum of intensity and an ambiguity that personhood cannot.

A Relational God

The God of the Old Testament is a God in relationship with His people. The creator in the Genesis accounts is always present with his creation. In Genesis 2, God talks to Adam and Eve, walks with them in the cool of the evening, and clothes them after their fall. Moreover, God recognizes Adam's need for relationship and, when he finds no partner among the animals, creates for him a mate, noting that "it is not good for the man to be alone" (2:18). After the fall, once humans and God no longer walk together, Genesis 4–9 presents a series of stories that show how badly things can go wrong when dominion over creation, through a variety of technologies, and relationship with God fall out of sync. The age-old struggle between the pastoralist and the technological cultivator of the land is explored in the story of Cain and Abel, and the relationship between siblings is shattered. The Tower of Babel, representing the move to urbanity, collapses, severing whole groups of people. Finally, in the story of the flood, Noah saves human and animal kind through the technology of the ark. The difference is that Noah enters the first of several covenants with God, a covenant that underlines humans as both in God's image and exercisers of dominion over the earth. Dominion without relationship to God, nature, and one another is a sure road to disaster.

But God's covenants are not just with individuals. William Dumbrell notes that a succession of interconnected covenants with Abraham, Moses, David, and, through the prophets, the

Israelite people as a whole, signal that God's care and concern are not merely for us as individuals. In the final analysis, God's plan for our redemption is a communal one. "Humanity finds its individual fullness in the blessedness of personal relationships."[52]

Barth finds an exemplar of the primacy of personal relationships in the life of Jesus, in whom he sees human nature as it was intended to be. What Barth considers significant about Jesus is his relationships, both with God and with his community:

> If we see Him alone, we do not see Him at all. If we see him, we see with and around Him in ever widening circles His disciples, the people, His enemies, and the countless multitudes who never have heard His name. We see Him as theirs, determined by them and for them, belonging to each and every one of them.[53]

For Barth, Jesus is both "man for God" in that he devotes himself exclusively to God's will and direction, and "man for other men" in the way he gives of himself in service to others.[54] With Jesus as our model, Barth notes that we, too, are seen and determined not just as individuals but in relationship to one another. Thus, all human beings are drawn into the covenant of grace that began with creation, and there is no possibility for human withdrawal from this covenant.

In his *Confessions*, Augustine famously writes, "You have made us for yourself, O Lord, and our hearts are restless until they rest in you."[55] Humankind is, in the words of Barth, "positively determined and filled in relationship to God."[56] In other words, we are "hard-wired" to be in relationship with someone or something not of the same essence as ourselves. Computer scientist Danny Hillis writes, "It would be nice to have friends that have a different set of limitations than we do. I would love to have one of my machines be such a friend."[57] Our striving for an AGI may hinge less on the desire to develop more useful servant technology than on our hope of creating something non-human with which we can relate. As Richard Forsyth and Chris Naylor put it:

> It can get lonely being conscious in the Cosmos—especially with people like Copernicus and Carl Sagan to tell you how big it is. Of course we can talk to each other, we can write books, but we are only talking to ourselves. After all, we are all human. Only four prospects of allaying this loneliness exist: (1) Communicating with extra-terrestrial intelligences. (2) Teaching animals to speak (e.g. chimpanzees). (3) Learning the language of another species (e.g. dolphins). (4) Building intelligent artifacts . . . It appears for the moment that if we want to contact a mind that is not housed in a human skull, we will have to build one.[58]

But if we build machines with which (or whom) we relate, what kind of relationship will that be?

Is It Authentic?

Christians believe that we can have a truly deep and authentic relationship with our Creator. What about with our creation? That we already have a relationship of sorts with various AIs (think Siri or Alexa) is not a question. But is this relationship closer to that of the young man with his car, or does it have the potential to grow into something mutual and mutually fulfilling?

Jewish theologian Martin Buber, in his 1923 classic *I and Thou*, lays out two types of relationships—the I-Thou and the I-It. The young man has an I-It relationship with his car. This is a stance where the I in the relationship treats the other as an object, to be used or experienced. We have I-It relationships with things, but we can also have such a relationship with people, whenever we objectify them or treat them as means to our own ends. The I-Thou relationship is one where, rather than the "I," the relationship itself is central. The Thou is met on its own terms and the boundaries between the two are diminished. Buber writes, "It exists only through being bounded by others . . . Thou has no bounds. When Thou is spoken, the speaker has no thing; he has indeed nothing. But he takes his stand in relation."[59]

Barth adopts Buber's I-Thou terminology. He describes the basic formula for an authentic encounter as "I am as Thou art."[60] Barth explains this phrase in reference first to God. He notes that "every 'I am' is qualified, marked, and determined" by the Thou who created it. We are reflections of our creator, of the creator's thoughts, talents, and intentions. Thus, we cannot fail to image God, just as AI cannot fail to image us in at least some respects. But Barth also notes that we are formed and marked not just by our Creator but by each and every authentic encounter with another.

What makes an encounter an authentic I-Thou encounter? Barth outlines four criteria. True encounter first demands that one "look the other in the eye."[61] By this, Barth means we recognize the other as both distinct from ourselves and as our true fellow. We are present to the other, not only physically but emotionally, open to mutual self-disclosure. We both see and are seen. This implies some form of physical presence. Indeed, Barth inveighs against "faceless bureaucracy" as the antithesis of authentic interaction. For AI, this criterion raises the question of embodiment. How much of today's so-called AI is a manifestation of Barth's bureaucracy, hiding and manipulating behind the scenes?

The second criterion is that we "speak to and hear one another." Barth notes the complexity of human speech and understanding, and while he does not limit mutual communication to the written or spoken word, he does feel that, for human beings, communication via some form of "the word" is a prerequisite for mutual self-disclosure, the vehicle through which we admit another into our own world. This speech act cannot be unidirectional and must result in mutual understanding: "I and Thou must both speak and hear, and speak with one another and hear one another. No element must be lacking."[62] Barth warns against the devaluation of words, recognizing that empty words lead to empty relationships that, ultimately, come from empty people.[63] When a robot speaks, from where do its words come? Can AI self-disclose, or is the self that is disclosed always at one remove?

Barth's third criterion involves action. We must "render mutual assistance." This calls for agency, the ability both to give and receive help, for Barth notes that "my humanity depends on the fact that I am always aware, and my action is determined by this awareness, that I need the assistance of others as a fish needs water. It depends upon my not being content with what I can do for myself, but calling for the Thou to give me the benefit of his action as well."[64] No one is an island. We need the assistance of others and are equally called to give the assistance others need. Why does Barth demand action for a full encounter? He writes, "If I and Thou really see each other and speak with one another and listen to one another, inevitably they mutually summon each other to action. . . . In the very fact that he lives, man calls to his fellow not to leave him alone or to his own devices . . . [to] spring to his side and give him a hand and actively stand by him."[65]

Finally, such help must be grounded in freedom and "offered gladly." Barth notes, "Companions are free. So are associates. So are comrades. So are fellows. So are helpmates."[66] After all, Jesus never said, "Go make others do things."[67] Our assistance must be neither grudging nor coerced. For a fully authentic encounter, it must be not only freely but "gladly" given. Not to do so would be, as Barth puts it, "reluctantly human."[68] Here we run into an issue with AI. Can anything programmed be said to be free? Are machines not coerced into helping us, and would we want it any other way? Finally, can a machine have emotions, or only simulate them? Is there any way for an AI to do something "gladly"?

In the next four chapters, we will explore each of Barth's criteria for authentic relationality in detail and examine how a relationship with an AI might or might not fulfill them. We will also consider how our computer-saturated and -mediated culture aids or hinders us in developing and sustaining authentic relationships with one another. Finally, we will encounter what, for Barth, is the central mystery and most profound contribution to the religious landscape by the Christian faith: the incarnation, death, and resurrection of Jesus. Barth insists that it is only through a consideration of the person of Jesus that we can grasp who God is and who we are meant to be. In taking on a human body, God became fully present to humanity. By enduring our suffering and mortality, God entered a fully authentic relationship with humankind. But what can suffering or mortality mean to a machine? Can we have a fulfilling relationship with something that does not share our embodied condition? We shall see.

Notes

1.   Rob Dozier, "This Clothing Line Was Designed By AI," *Vice*, June 3, 2019, https://tinyurl.com/z5sva5tc.

2.   Matt Simon, "Your Online Shopping Habit Is Fueling a Robotics Renaissance," *Wired*, December 6, 2017, https://tinyurl.com/2p859yrb.

3.   James Vincent, "DeepMind's AI Can Detect over 50 Eye Diseases as Accurately as a Doctor," *The Verge*, August 13, 2018, https://tinyurl.com/22nzyta8.

4.   Brian X. Chen and Cade Metz, "Google's Duplex Uses AI to Mimic Humans (Sometimes)," *New York Times*, May 22, 2019, https://tinyurl.com/3h2uuww5.

5. Michael Laris, "Waymo Launches Nation's First Commercial Self-Driving Taxi Service in Arizona." *Washington Post*, December 5, 2018, https://tinyurl.com/53t7bnr7.

6. Tonya Riley, "Get Ready, This Year Your next Job Interview May Be with an AI Robot," *CNBC*, March 13, 2018, https://tinyurl.com/2p8nnzfy.

7. Rachel O'Dwyer, "Algorithms Are Making the Same Mistakes as Humans Assessing Credit Scores." *Quartz*, May 14, 2018, https://tinyurl.com/mu8s62k3.

8. Christopher Rigano, "Using Artificial Intelligence to Address Criminal Justice Needs," National Institute of Justice, October 8, 2018, https://tinyurl.com/y7xt969x.

9. As one investor noted, "Sure, that might lead to a dystopian future or something, but you can't ban it." Michelle Goldberg, "The Darkness Where the Future Should Be," *New York Times*, January 24, 2020, https://tinyurl.com/mtwrtrtp.

10. Paul Mozur, "One Month, 500,000 Face Scans: How China Is Using AI to Profile a Minority," *New York Times*, April 14, 2019, https://tinyurl.com/2p9cs632.

11. Robert S. Muller III, "Report on the Investigation into Russian Interference in the 2016 Presidential Election," March 2019, 448, https://tinyurl.com/4ankws2h.

12. Matthew Martinez, "'Sex robot brothel' coming to Houston, Texas, and it's legal," September 25, 2018, https://tinyurl.com/2kzdf63n.

13. "Silicone Soul: A Documentary by Melody Gilbert," accessed June 10, 2019, https://tinyurl.com/mscx945w.

14. Sherry Turkle, *Alone Together: Why We Expect More from Technology and Less from Each Other* (New York: Basic Books, 2011), 12.

15. "Sophia," Hanson Robotics, accessed June 7, 2019, https://tinyurl.com/ykbsv8fv.

16. Andrew Griffin, "Stephen Hawking: Artificial Intelligence Could Wipe Out Humanity When It Gets Too Clever as Humans Will Be Like Ants," *Independent*, October 8, 2015, https://tinyurl.com/2p9yhvva.

17. Matt McFarland, "Elon Musk: 'With artificial intelligence we are summoning the demon,'" *Washington Post*, October 24, 2014, https://tinyurl.com/5n9a55vz.

18. James Moor, "The Dartmouth College Artificial Intelligence Conference: The Next Fifty Years," *AI Magazine*, Vol 27:4, December 15, 2006, 87, https://tinyurl.com/545zsfts.

19. David Gelernter, *The Muse in the Machine: Computerizing the Poetry of Human Thought* (New York: Free Press, 1994), 44.

20. Marvin Minsky, *Semantic Information Processing* (Cambridge, MA: MIT Press, 1968).

21. *Jacobellis vs. Ohio*, 378 US 184 (1964) Supreme Court decision.

22. Herbert Simon, "Modeling Human Mental Processes" (paper presented at the Western Joint IRE-AIEE-ACM Computer Conference, Los Angeles, California, May 9–11, 1961), 111–9, https://tinyurl.com/2p8mjrzf.

23. Herbert Simon and Allen Newell, "Computer Science as Empirical Inquiry: Symbols and Search" in *Mind Design II: Philosophy, Psychology, Artificial Intelligence*, ed. John Haugeland (Cambridge MA: MIT, 1997), 87.

24. Ludwig Wittgenstein, *Tractatus Logico-Philosophicus* (London: Routledge and Kegan Paul, 1960), 1.1, 2.01.

25. Thomas Hobbes, *Leviathan* (New York: Library of Liberal Arts, 1958), 45.

26. Although it seems like a big *if* to assume that consciousness arises out a process of symbol manipulation, the hypothesis that this is precisely how our minds operate is widely accepted in the scientific community. See, for example, Francis Crick, *The Astonishing Hypothesis: The Scientific Search for the Soul* (New York: Scribner's, 1994) or Daniel Dennett, *Consciousness Explained* (Boston: Little, Brown, 1991). Of course, the digital computer did not exist in the 1930s. Alonzo Church formulated the thesis that any problem that can be solved with a finite algorithm can be solved using a Turing machine, a mathematical model proposed by Alan Turing on which the logical functioning of the computer is based. Turing proposed that his model could be programmed to mimic any conceivable computational device. The combined suggestion that the digital computer represents a realization of the Turing machine, and can be programmed to carry out any consistent, terminating algorithm, is the Turing-Church hypothesis and is accepted as valid, though unprovable, by most computer scientists.

27. For a discussion of programming methods in game playing, see Nils Nilsson, *Artificial Intelligence: A New Synthesis* (San Francisco: Morgan Kaufmann, 1998), 139–215.

28. Hubert Dreyfus and Stuart Dreyfus, "Making a Mind versus Modeling the Brain: Artificial Intelligence Back at a Branchpoint." *Daedalus* 117, no. 1 (1988): 32.

29. Brad Darrach, "Meet Shaky, the first electronic person," *Life*, November 20, 1970, https://tinyurl.com/4brm3fhw.

30. Or, perhaps I should say "questions."

31. "Husky or Wolf? Using a Black Box Learning Model to Avoid Adoption Errors," *UCI Beall Applied Innovation,* August 24, 2017, https://tinyurl.com/ymr4wtbj.

32. Jean-Claude Beaune, *L'Automate et ses Mobiles* (Paris: Flammarion, 1980), 38.

33. Daniel Crevier, *AI: The Tumultuous History of the Search for Artificial Intelligence* (New York: Basic Books, 1993), 2–3.

34. David Cairnes, *The Image of God in Man*, with Introduction by David E. Jenkins, Fontana Library of Theology and Philosophy (London: SCM, 1953; reprint, London: Collins, 1973), 60.

35. Early Christian writers who discuss the *imago Dei* in terms of reason or the rational mind include Clement of Alexandria (*Stromateis* 5.14), Origen (*Against Celsus* 4.85), Gregory of Nazianzus (*Orations* 38.11), Gregory of Nyssa (*On the Making of Man* 5), and Augustine (*On the Trinity* 12–14).

36. Carl F. H. Henry, ed., *Baker's Dictionary of Christian Ethics* (Grand Rapids MI: Baker, 1973), s. v. "Image of God," by Gordon H. Clark. Clark also gives a Christological argument for reason as the *imago Dei*, based on the understanding of Christ as the Logos or Wisdom of God. Sin is understood as either incomplete knowledge or a malfunctioning of the mind. Clark remarks that in heaven, we will no longer make mistakes, "even in arithmetic." In this case, computers have perhaps brought us a bit of heaven on earth!

37. Johannes Hehn, "Zum Terminus 'Bild Gottes,'" in *Festschrift Eduard Sachau zum siebzigsten Geburtstag* (Berlin: G. Reimer, 1915), 36–52.

38. Wilhelm Caspari advanced a similar theory in his 1929 article, "Imago divina Gen I," in *Festschrift R. Seeberg: Zur Theorie des Christentums* (Leipzig, 1929).

39. Gerhard von Rad, *Genesis: A Commentary*, trans. John H. Marks, The Old Testament Library (Philadelphia: Westminster, 1961), 56.

40. von Rad, *Genesis*, 58.

41. Karl Barth, *Church Dogmatics*, vol. 3, *The Doctrine of Creation Part 2*, ed. Geoffrey Bromiley, Thomas Torrance, trans. J. W. Edwards, O. Bussey, Harold Knight (Edinburgh: T&T Clark, 1958), 184–5. Barth lists and denies the variety of actions that we might consider in such a list as ever being enough to constitute a valid image: "The fact that I am born and die; that I act and drink and sleep; that I develop and maintain myself; that beyond this I assert myself in the face of others, and even physically propagate my sperm; that I enjoy and work and play and fashion and possess; that I acquire and have and exercise powers; that I take part in all the work of the race; and that in it all I fulfill my aptitudes as an understanding and thinking, willing and feeling being—all this is not my humanity." *Church Dogmatics*, 249.

42. Barth, *Church Dogmatics*, 3:182.

43. See, for example Ross Andersen, "Scientists are Totally Rethinking Animal Cognition," *The Atlantic*, March 2019, https://tinyurl.com/2pkvdpce.

Barth himself was agnostic as to whether animals had a relationship with God, stating that without better communication, we really could not know.

44. Douglas Hall, *Imaging God: Dominion as Stewardship* (Grand Rapids: Eerdmans, 1986), 124.

45. James Manyika, et al., "A Future that Works: Automation, Employment, and Productivity," McKinsey Global Institute, January 12, 2017, https://tinyurl.com/2p9cu3ph.

46. Alan Turing, "Computing Machinery and Intelligence," *Mind*, 49 (1950), 433–60. René Descartes prefigured Turing in his suggestion that discourse would distinguish machines from humans. In his *Discourse on Method* (found in Keith Gunderson, "Descartes, La Mettrie, Language and Machines," *Philosophy*, 39 (1964), 193–222), he writes,

> If there were machines which bore a resemblance to our bodies and imitated our actions as closely as possible for all practical purposes, we should still have two very certain means of recognizing that they were not real men. The first is that they could never use words, or put together signs, as we do in order to declare our thoughts to others. For we can certainly conceive of a machine so constructed that it utters words, and even utters words that correspond to bodily actions causing a change in its organs. . . . But it is not conceivable that such a machine should produce different arrangements of words so as to give an appropriately meaningful answer to whatever is said in its presence, as the dullest of men can do.

47. Turing, "Computing Machinery and Intelligence," 442.

48. This is not to say that machines are not frequently mistaken for humans. In 2017 Twitter's congressional deposition estimated that 5 percent of its accounts were bots. Independent researchers suggest that percentage may be as high as 15 percent, and that we humans are not very good at distinguishing the bots from real humans. But Twitter is a much more artificial environment than Turing envisioned. Onur Varol, et al., "Online Human-Bot Interactions: Detection, Estimation, and Characterization," *Proceedings of the International AAAI Conference on Web and Social Media* 11, no. 1 (201): 280–89.

49. Alan Turing, "Computing Machinery and Intelligence," *Mind* LIX, no. 236 (October 1, 1950): 433–60, https://tinyurl.com/2zrsc377.

50. Sophia is a human-like robot created by Hansen Robotics to copy human facial expressions, gestures, and speech patterns. For a description and video, see "Sophia," Hanson Robotics, https://tinyurl.com/2p9cu3ph.

51. For a deeper dive into AI and personhood, see Gunkel, D. J. and Wales, J. J., "Debate: what is personhood in the age of AI?" *AI & Soc* 36 (2021): 473–86 https://doi.org/10.1007/s00146-020-01129-1.

52. William Dumbrell, *Covenant and Creation: An Old Testament Covenant Theology* (Milton Keynes: Authentic Media, 2013), 6.

53. Dumbrell, *Covenant and Creation*, 216.

54. Dumbrell, *Covenant and Creation*, 63–4, 213.

55. Augustine, Confessions (Book 1, 2.5,5).

56. Barth, *Church Dogmatics*, 3:130.

57. Quoted in David Noble, *The Religion of Technology: The Divinity of Man and the Spirit of Invention* (New York: Knopf, 1997), 170.

58. Richard Forsyth and Chris Naylor, *The Hitch-Hiker's Guide to Artificial Intelligence* (London: Chapman and Hall/Methuen, 1986), 245.

59. Martin Buber, *I and Thou* (United Kingdom: Free Press, 1996). Buber follows Immanuel Kant's categorical imperative that we should always treat others as ends rather than means. He takes this one step further by suggesting that we can have an I-Thou relationship with an object so long as we accept that object as existing for itself rather than for our instrumental use.

60. Buber, *I and Thou*, 248.

61. Barth, *Church Dogmatics*, 3:250.

62. Barth, *Church Dogmatics*, 3:252.

63. Barth, *Church Dogmatics*, 3:260.

64. Barth, *Church Dogmatics*, 3:263.

65. Barth, *Church Dogmatics*, 3:261–2.

66. Barth, *Church Dogmatics*, 3:271.

67. Frederick Schmidt, "Jesus Never Said, 'Go Make Others Do Things.'" *What God Wants for Your Life*, June 7, 2019, https://tinyurl.com/nhc55a6k.

68. Schmidt, "Jesus Never Said."

2

Do We Need Bodies?

"I have looked into your eyes with my eyes.
I have put my heart near your heart."

—Pope John XXIII

This morning I made three appointments, one over the phone and two online. With Google Duplex, a personal assistant app, I could have had my computer do this for me, and the receptionists at the other end would have never known they were talking with a machine rather than a human. As I go out to run errands later this morning, I might accomplish all I need to do without seeing another human being, as I pump my own gas, use the ATM, check out my own groceries, and get a book from the library.

Nor are these scenarios the only ways automation makes face-to-face communication unnecessary. Among my students, texting is the preferred mode of communication. As one student explained, a text seems less rude than a phone call since it does not demand an immediate response. When I enter my classroom these days, it is not uncommon for the room to be silent, all heads bent over a laptop or smartphone. Though inches away from each other, my students converse with someone at a safe remove. One noted, "It's a way to hide." During the pandemic, I "saw" my students over Zoom. But many preferred to turn off their cameras while they lounged in bed or walked the dog. I saw only their name in a black box.

And this is precisely the problem. For Barth, the first criterion for an authentic relationship requires us not to hide but to look the other in the eye. MIT sociologist Sherry Turkle agrees. "Face-to-face conversation" she argues, "is the most human—and humanizing—thing we do. Fully present to one another we learn to listen. It's where we develop the capacity for empathy. It's where we experience the joy of being heard, of being understood."[1] Looking the other in the eye is thus not just one criterion among others but the bedrock of Barth's other criteria. We cannot fully listen, hear and be heard, understand and empathize, and give aid unless we are physically present to one another. It is not that we cannot do these things from a distance, it is rather that we cannot do them in their fullness. It is only face to face that we completely apprehend the being of the other and, subsequently, our duty to them. Emmanuel Levinas posits recognition of the "face" of the other as the starting point for a moral life. He writes, "The Other becomes my neighbor precisely through the way the face summons me, calls for me, begs for me, and in so doing recalls my responsibility, and calls me into question."[2]

We apprehend the world through our senses, and, for humans, our primary sense is sight. To look the other in the eye is to apprehend the other at their most basic level. As the saying has it, "seeing is believing." I acknowledge you as a separate being with a life and volition of your own when I look you in the eye. To look "in the eye" is also to establish a form of mutuality. If I am servile, I will not look so high; if I consider myself superior, I may not look at you at all. In the act of looking each other in the eye we acknowledge a certain equality of being and engagement. It is also an acknowl-edgement of something deeper. The eyes are said to be windows to the soul. When we look another in the eye, we experience the other in a way that goes beyond factual comprehension.

But must we take *face* or *eye* literally? Does an artificial intel-ligence need to have a face for us to fully relate to it? What about all our texts, social media posts, tweets, and interactions on video games? Do these not establish our presence to one another without a face? Do we really need face-to-face encounters to be, as Turkle suggests, fully human? In other words, could intelligence, even our own minds, exist without a body?

The Ghost in the Machine

"Well, that ought to keep body and soul together," my father would say after a particularly good meal. Keeping body and soul, or mind, together has heretofore been a given. But no longer. Many transhu-manists envision a not-too-distant future in which technology and neuroscience converge to allow us a purely mental existence. Futur-ist Ray Kurzweil envisions scanning a brain's neural structure and instantiating it in "a suitably powerful computational substrate," thus capturing "a person's entire personality, memory, skills, and history."[3] Once our "self" is ported to a silicon platform, we will no longer be limited by our physical bodies. Kurzweil writes:

> Up until now, our mortality was tied to the longevity of our hardware. When the hardware crashed, that was it. . . . As we cross the divide to instantiate ourselves into our compu-tational technology, our identity will be based on our evolv-ing mind file. We will be software, not hardware. . . . As software, our mortality will no longer be dependent on the survival of the computing circuitry . . . [as] we periodically

port ourselves to the latest, evermore capable "personal" computer. . . . Our immortality will be a matter of being sufficiently careful to make frequent backups.[4]

This dream of a cybernetic immortality assumes that our essential self consists of our memories and thoughts, which are nothing more than patterns stored in the neural connections of our brain. If this is so, it would seem possible for these patterns to be replicated on a different platform, recreating the essence of a person without the physical body.

Or we could design a mind that never had a body. Computer scientist Hans Moravec suggests that artificial intelligences will become our "mind children," the next step in an evolutionary process geared toward maximizing intelligence. He envisions a future in which life will come to inhabit, first, bodies of silicon and metal, but later, no body at all. Our mind children would exist in cyberspace, rather than real space, either independently, as avatars, or merged into a single "extended thinking entity."[5] Philosopher David Chalmers envisions a similar future. "At some point I think we must face the fact that there are going to be many faster substrates for running intelligence than our own. If we want to stick to our biological brains, then we are in danger of being left behind in a world with superfast, superintelligent computers."[6]

Most scientists and philosophers who envision a cybernetic future are not religious. They are looking to the computer as the only means, in a strictly material universe, to surmount death. But there are also religious transhumanists. Calvin Mercer finds the apostle Paul's assertion in 1 Corinthians that that dead will be raised with new bodies to be congruent with cybernetic immortality, since "the post-resurrection body is qualitatively different from the 'flesh and blood' body."[7] At first glance, this idea of a person in a machine looks a lot like Cartesian mind-body dualism. A soul or mind that sits, sometimes uneasily, on top of the substratum of the body was foundational to Descartes's thinking. Unlike Descartes, however, today's futurists consider the soul, which they correlate with the mind, as post-existent rather than pre-existent, arising from the body and the skills and memories that body provides, yet separable from that body at some point in time.

The idea that a body and a mind can exist separately was foundational to the earliest attempts to create AI. As we saw in chapter one, symbolic AI attempted to create computer models of different aspects of cognition, and then to manipulate those models. This method worked quite well in the limited environments of virtual worlds, such as those of most games. But symbolic AI proved hopelessly inadequate in the real world, failing at the sort of things a three-year-old child easily masters, such as language, facial recognition, and simply navigating across a crowded room.

But wait, you are thinking, *Can't computers do all those things today?* Through the bottom-up approach of machine learning, computers now not only beat all comers at chess, Jeopardy!, and Go, but they also answer most of our questions, guide us to our destinations, read lips, compose pop hits, and modify their own programs. Robots can navigate even rough terrain. But they have their limits. Since their famous chess match, Garry Kasparov has used what he learned of strategy at the chess table to become a political thorn in Russian President Vladimir Putin's side, but his opponent Deep Blue, like most narrow systems, designed only to play chess (indeed, only to play Kasparov), could do nothing else and has now been decommissioned. We are still a long way from creating a general intelligence that can bring learning from one area into many others.

Ben Medlock, cofounder of SwiftKey, a voice-to-text system, believes the problem is precisely the lack of a body. He notes that "long before we were conscious, thinking beings, our cells were reading data from the environment and working together to mould us into robust, self-sustaining agents. What we take as intelligence, then, is not simply about using symbols to represent the world as it objectively is. Rather, we only have the world as it is revealed to us, which is rooted in our evolved, embodied needs as an organism."[8] He believes the imperative of bodily survival in a complex and ever-changing world provides the ground for the flexibility and power of our minds, noting that "our body and brain, from the cellular level upwards, have already built a model of the world that we can apply almost instantly to a wide array of challenges."[9] While some computer scientists, such as Rodney Brooks, have accepted that the best avenue to AI might be through designing robotic beings that similarly learn through immersion in their environment, most are still trying to build AI programs starting with a specific problem or application for which they develop a portable—and thus, disembodied—solution.

While a disembodied mind is a source of hope for transhumanists and AI entrepreneurs, it has been a source of horror in folklore and literature. A soul without a body, and the converse, a body without a soul, have been staple themes of horror films and the late-night stories children scare each other with around the campfire. A soul without a body is a ghost; a body without a soul is a zombie. Zombies first appear in popular culture in the 1920s. Since the turn of the century, they have shambled out of grade-B film into the mainstream. A sampling of recent titles gives a taste of their popularity: *Dawn of the Dead* (2004), *Little Monsters* (2019), *Army of the Dead* (2021), *Train to Busan* (2016), and Brad Pitt's *World War Z* (2013). There are zombie video games, such as *Resident Evil* and *Left for Dead*. and television programs, such as *The Walking Dead*. True to their nature, zombies have become a meme that refuses to die.[10] Max Brooks, author of *Zombie Survival Guide*, suggests zombies present an outlet for the fears and anxieties that plague our culture: "You can't shoot the financial meltdown in the head—you can do that with a zombie . . . All the other problems are too big. As much as Al Gore tries, you can't picture global warming. You can't picture the meltdown of our financial institutions. But you can picture a slouching zombie coming down the street."[11]

The idea of a soul without a body has a much longer pedigree. Animism, the peopling of the physical world with souls or spirits, allows human-like rationality and agency to reside in nonhuman and even inorganic bodies. A tree may have a soul. So, too, might a spring or even the wind. These are not human spirits; rather, they are spirits intrinsic to and defined by that in which they reside. It is in the ghost that we find a human consciousness acting in the world without a body. Like the zombie, the ghost is frightening in that it, too, cannot die. But while the zombie can do nothing more than stalk mindlessly across the land and consume, the ghost can reason, communicate, and act in ways both malign and benign; thus, ghosts seem far less alien than zombies. Ghost stories give us a thrill that is equally chilling and pleasurable. Indeed, some try to contact the disembodied souls of loved ones. Others maintain a ghostlike existence for the dead on Facebook pages. Whether on social media or in a seance, communication with the dead rests in part on the folk perception of the dead as disembodied souls, able to both monitor what occurs on earth and to partake in some sort of alternative world. Transhumanists who dream of separating the mind from the body hope to produce through technology just such a ghostlike existence, turning us, or our successors, into bodyless spirits inhabiting a procession of machines, able to know what happens in the real world while also experiencing a variety of virtual worlds.

Why Not Ghosts?

The ability to transfer the human mind to a computer rests on the assumption expressed most clearly by Nobel Laureate Francis Crick: "You, your joys and your sorrows, your memories and your ambitions, your sense of personal identity and free will, are in fact no more than the behavior of a vast assembly of nerve cells and their associated molecules . . . You're nothing but a pack of neurons."[12] Crick posits that the self is the product of our neuronal patterns and their functioning. We are, in essence, information, and information is always reducible to patterns of zeros and ones. This position is appealing in an age in which everything is rapidly becoming digitalized. It provides a simple model for human identity and individuality; we are each a unique pattern. Kurzweil begins with an assumption much like Crick's: "So who am I? Since I am constantly changing, am I just a pattern? What if someone copies that pattern? Am I the original and/or the copy? Perhaps I am this stuff here—that is, the both ordered and chaotic collection of molecules that make up my body and brain."[13] However, noting the ever-changing nature of these molecules, Kurzweil dismisses the molecules of the body and settles instead on the underlying pattern as the source of our identity:

> We know that most of our cells are turned over in a matter of weeks, and even our neurons, which persist as distinct cells for a relatively long time, nonetheless change all of their constituent molecules within a month . . . I am rather like the pattern that water makes in a stream as it rushes past the rocks in its path. The actual molecules of water change every millisecond, but the pattern persists for hours or even years.[14]

Moravec, seeking to avoid the duplication problem Kurzweil notes as inherent in identity as a pattern, envisions replacing one neuron after another in our brain with transistors, until the brain is entirely made up of a circuitry structure in the exact pattern of the original neurons.[15] Still, there is no reason, once a digital version of a brain exists, not to copy it, hence, the duplication problem reappears.

There are several other problems with this conception of the human being as pattern. First, it is vastly oversimplified. Our brains are more than neurons and their connections. Our neural connections are both enabled and inhibited by a variety of neurochemicals such as serotonin, dopamine, and oxytocin. These chemicals allow for a variety of firing thresholds and receptions, making the firing of a neuron more complex than a simple binary on or off. These chemicals and their enhancing or restraining effects would need some sort of presence in the pattern, at minimum, as variables in the algorithms that govern neural connections. Furthermore, spontaneous fluctuations occur in which neurons fire even when no external stimulus or mental cogitation has occurred, and these spontaneous fluctuations make up almost 95 percent of brain activity. Our neurons are continually firing, but we do not yet know why, nor how this affects our thoughts or consciousness.[16] Neuroscientist Stanislas Dehaene wonders whether these fluctuations, long dismissed as simply "noise" in the system, are not, in fact, a feature rather than a bug. He notes that our "neurons not only tolerate noise but even amplify it," and this may be one source of our consciousness or our ability to intuit novel solutions to a problem.[17]

Then there is the fact that the brain represents only part of our neurological system. Hundreds of millions of neurons connect our brains to our enteric nervous system, which can be called our "second brain." Cues from brain to stomach manage digestion (something a computerized version of the self could presumably do without). However, communication between the brain and the gut goes in both directions. Research at the Karolinska Institute in Sweden and the Genome Institute of Singapore has shown that the bacteria in our gut can influence both brain development and adult behavior. While we are only beginning to understand the import of our microbiota, a complete model of the human mind would need to simulate brain, gut, and the millions of bacteria that inhabit the gut.[18]

How close are we to being able to map our brain's neural connections? Sebastian Seung is one of the leaders of the Human Connectome Project, which is attempting to produce precisely such a map using MRI scans. Yet he admits his hopes are, at times, tinged with despair when he contemplates the magnitude of the project. The human brain contains approximately 80–90 billion neurons, each of which has the potential to be connected to several thousand other neurons. Nor are these connections permanent, but continually changing. Seung estimates that imaging the brain with ordinary electron microscopes will produce one zettabyte of data, the equivalent of all data currently stored on the internet. So far, he has looked for payoff through the modeling of much smaller regions and structures within the brain, models that might give us some insight into various brain disorders.[19]

A model like Seung's might well let us see the differences between a healthy and an unhealthy brain. What is not clear is whether it would give us any insight into what makes a thought, a discovery that is crucial to Kurzweil and Moravec's dream of reinstantiation. While we currently understand the functioning of a single neuron or small group of neurons and can use MRI machines and PET scans to map blood flow to large regions of the brain, giving some idea of what a person may be thinking or feeling in a highly restrictive setting, we do not understand the middle ground, the functioning of large chains of neurons, nor do we have any idea how these chains represent thoughts or memories. And this challenge does not even consider the underlying ontological question of whether a copy of the brain's structure would retain any operativity.

While these technological difficulties might someday be surmounted, there remain concerns. Physicist Michio Kaku worries that a brain without a sufficiently human body might suffer the effects of sensory isolation similar to those experienced by prisoners in solitary confinement. He writes, "perhaps the price of creating an immortal, reverse-engineered brain is madness."[20] Transhumanist philosopher Nick Bostrom disagrees. "An upload," he writes, "could have a virtual (simulated) body giving the same sensations and the same possibilities for interaction as a non-simulated body. . . . For the continuation of personhood, on this view, it matters little whether you are implemented on a silicon chip inside a computer or in that gray, cheesy lump inside your skull, assuming both implementations are conscious."[21]

Now we're talking about simulating the whole body. And while the uploaded brain could be attached to an array of sensors allowing it contact with the outside world, as Bostrom proposes, the input from those sensors would differ greatly from the input that the mind was used to receiving through the physical senses. If the essence of the human personality were maintained in the uploading process, the reproduced mind would still crave physical human contact. Would a virtual existence provide the kind of contact we need? Kaku notes that when given the choice between "high tech" and "high touch," we almost always choose the latter.[22] Any simulation of the brain would need to be accompanied with a highly detailed simulation of the body's sensory inputs as well, vastly increasing the complexity of an already complex project.

"I'm as fond of my body as anyone," quips computer scientist Daniel Hill, "but if I can be 200 in a body of silicon, I'll take it."[23]

However, while we can imagine an existence without our aging and fallible bodies, when examined closely, such an existence might be just as dissatisfying as the ancient Greeks and Hebrews imagined the ghostly existence of the shades in Hades or Sheol to be. To them, the prospect of an afterlife without a body was not a happy one. Our Christian forbears instinctively recognized that a fully human identity requires bodily existence within an environment. An immortality that would continue anything like the human life we have known and anything like the selves that we are must be instantiated in a human body. Thus, though many Christians speak as if they were functional dualists, believing that only their soul goes to heaven after death, the Apostles' Creed states that we believe in "the resurrection of the body and life everlasting."

More Zombie Than Ghost

Rather than a ghost-like existence in a machine, a likelier outcome is that the uploaded or manufactured brain would retain the ability to calculate but lose human consciousness and *qualia*—the ability to feel—thus becoming more zombie than ghost. A zombie, or body without a soul, describes the current field of robotics. Robots possess bodies. We can look them in the eye. But are robotic eyes windows to robotic souls? Our current robots are not conscious. They do not internalize experience as we do. Whether they someday will be is unclear, not just because of the technological challenges involved but because we have no idea what, exactly, consciousness is. Chalmers calls consciousness "the hard problem" for AI, and believes the problem of experience will persist even if we attain a functional model of all relevant parts of the brain: "It is widely agreed that experience arises from a physical basis, but we have no good explanation of why and how it so arises."[24] We have no idea how to make a machine experience subjectivity.

Nick Bostrom believes simulating a mind does not require complete human cognition, noting that emulation of a complete human brain is a daunting task. He suggests, rather, that "the aim is not to create a brain simulation so detailed and accurate that one could use it to predict exactly what would have happened in the original brain" but to "aim to capture enough of the computationally functional properties of the brain to enable the resultant emulation to perform intellectual work."[25] This description fits the trajectory of present robotic technology and avoids the hard problem of consciousness. Robots provide us with an emulation of an embodied person but fall far short of the real thing. They can emulate human activities and achievements. They can look us in the eye. But we know that there is no one home behind that gaze.

Barth notes that true seeing demands mutuality: "To see the other is to let oneself be seen by him. . . . The two together constitute the full human significance of the eye and its seeing. All seeing is inhuman in which the one who sees hides himself refusing to be seen by the fellow-man whom he sees."[26] Is such mutuality possible with a robot? There are limitations on both sides. We may look the robot in the eye without any real knowledge of what we are seeing. To see the other is to gain understanding of something foundational and immutable in the other. Robots are entirely mutable. The next time we see the same robot, its programming may have been completely changed. Does the robot see us? It may, through facial recognition, identify us the next time we meet. It may even make a sophisticated analysis of our expression, our words, and have a great deal of data about our past on which it can draw. But to what extent does this constitute the openness to the other Barth demands? For Barth, in seeing the other, we acknowledge "I am as Thou art." Yet we and the robot are not the same.

Living as Ghosts Online

Today we outsource more and more of our mental activities to our smart phones and devices. It is no coincidence that rise has paralleled the use of ghosts and zombies as plot devices in literature and film. It is hard for me not to think of zombies as I watch students shambling across campus, bent over their phones, oblivious to everything and everyone around them. While acting like a zombie to those in the same physical space, they are ghosts to those with whom they communicate. More and more of our lives happen in this ghostly virtual world. Virginia Heffernan notes that this shift in attention "stirs grief: the deep feeling that digitization has cost us something very profound," through alienation from voices and bodies that can find comfort in each other. Digital connectedness, she concludes, "is illusory; . . . we're all more alone than ever."[27] Yet the virtual world remains highly seductive. My students say it is "safer" than the real world. And during the Covid-19 pandemic, it was. But it was also far lonelier. The French philosopher and mystic Simone Weil wrote of our reluctance to look the other in the eye: "Something in our soul has a far more violent repugnance for true attention than the flesh has for bodily fatigue. That something is more closely connected to evil than is the flesh. That is why, every time we truly give our attention, we destroy some evil in ourselves."[28] Relationships in cyberspace, established and maintained through texts and posts, fail Barth's criterion of looking the other in the eye—this first and most basic sensory apprehension of the other's being is missing. Why does this matter?

First, I do not know if you are human. In a famous cartoon in *The New Yorker*, one dog sitting in front of a computer says to another, "On the internet, nobody knows you're a dog."[29] When almost 100 million active users on Facebook are bots, chances are quite likely that each of us is regularly interacting with machines we assume to be human. In a 2017 *Atlantic* article entitled "The Internet Is Mostly Bots," Adrienne LaFrance noted that when the security firm Imperva analyzed nearly 17 billion website visits from across 100,000 domains, it found that bots were responsible for at least 52 percent of web traffic. "For the past five years, every third website visitor was an attack bot" and 90 percent of the websites analyzed had had an interaction with a bot.[30] Companies like Facebook and Twitter use machine learning programs to detect and flag bots, but have had limited success in stopping them given their rapid evolution. Once a bot gets through the filters, we humans are terrible at detecting them. And the problem is only getting worse. AI research firm OpenAI has developed a program, GPT-3, capable of writing text to mimic any human writer in both style and substance. So far, the company has refrained from releasing the program to the public, fearing its potential for malicious misuse, but it is only a matter of time before this technology, or something like it, is deployed.[31] Just as AI can now produce "deep fake" videos showing things that never happened, deep fake text is on the way. And on the internet, they will not know you're a bot.

But what about human users? Is the person we access on social media really who we think they are? A survey of over 2000 people in the UK found that more than three-quarters of the respondents admitted to lying on their social profiles, and only 18 percent said their Facebook or Twitter posts accurately represented their lives.[32] We post pictures of our younger selves, lie about our ages and weights, and reveal only our best moments. This curation has repercussions. Sociologists Jean Twenge and Jonathan Haidt have documented a pronounced rise in unhappiness and mental health issues among today's young people. Studies show more screen time correlates with higher rates of depression, while more in-person social interaction correlates with greater happiness. Time online means less time attending to the physical world. According to Twenge, "College students in 2016 (vs. the late 1980s) spent four fewer hours a week socializing with their friends and three fewer hours a week partying—so seven hours a week less on in-person social interaction."[33]

We all experienced the loss of physical presence when our lives moved online during the pandemic. Students who missed a trip to the cathedral at Chartres but viewed a 3D rendering online, even one specific in detail, felt cheated. How deeply we sympathized with those who had to say goodbye to loved ones dying of Covid through iPads held by harried nurses. We can look at someone's eyes on a screen, but something is lost. It is hard to feel a true connection. Nor can we hold their hand. A hug engaged in by two avatars is not a hug. Touch is vital for human flourishing. Infants cannot survive without human touch. Skin-to-skin contact after birth regulates the newborn's temperature, heart rate, and breathing, and relaxes the new mother. Children deprived of touch in Romanian orphanages remained underdeveloped, both mentally and physically.[34] In adults, the touch of another human, or even a pet, lowers blood pressure, heart rate, and cortisol levels. Holding another's hand quiets the stress mechanisms of the brain, even if the hand being held is that of a stranger.[35]

Levinas notes an importance to physical presence that goes beyond the body's ability to express and communicate our inner state. He writes that, "the spirituality of the body does not lie in this power to express what is inward. By its position it realizes the condition necessary for any inwardness. It does not express an event; it is itself this event."[36] In times of grief or tragedy, we hold someone's hand, we weep tears along with theirs, and it is the very physicality of these actions that conveys our human solidarity and empathy. Indeed, often the only thing we can offer the bereaved is our physical presence.

A robot, despite having a physical presence, lacks one further means of interaction and communication. We communicate not only through words, gestures, body language, and facial expressions but also through smell. This communication occurs subconsciously, and it can override more conscious signals. When asked once why I was attracted to a particular boyfriend who seemed to share few of my values, I could only say *He smells good*. His aroma had nothing to do with soap or aftershave. Our bodies emit pheromones that send signals regarding interest in the other, sexual status, aggression, and even one's position in the social hierarchy.[37] These signals tell us something about a person's health, their microbiota, and even their compatibility for reproduction with our own bodies. This explains why some couples who imagine themselves in love with someone they have met online are deeply disappointed when they finally meet in person only to find that there is no "chemistry" between them. Physical presence adds a depth and nuance to our interactions that is lost when those interactions are mediated by computers, no matter how immersive the application or high the resolution.

The Narcissism of Ghosts and Zombies

We tend to think of narcissism as a failing that is particular to those who value their bodies too highly. The mythological Narcissus was captivated by the beauty of his own reflection. But it is not only the reflection of the body that can captivate us. So, too, can the reflection of the mind. Narcissism is a pitfall for transhumanists who imagine a "ghostly" existence outside the "death trap" of the body. The transhumanist who wishes to upload his mind to a computer must answer one final question—why should *his* mind persist? What is so important about *her* thoughts, values, memories, or experiences that they should be retained? In *The Culture of Narcissism*, Christopher Lasch suggests that our intense anxiety over aging and death turns us into grasping overconsumers, who overconsume not just material goods but life itself. Ray Kurzweil epitomizes this tendency, following a stringent dietary and exercise routine, including taking more than 150 supplements a day in the hope of living until our technology has developed sufficiently to allow brain uploading. Other transhumanists are counting on cryogenics, freezing their brains in hopes that their neural patterns might be available for copying at some point in time. This grasping at life is in direct contradiction to the words and example of Jesus, that "whoever wishes to save his life will lose it, but whoever loses his life for my sake, he is the one who will save it." (Luke 9:24)

In the writings of those who desire cybernetic immortality, it is always "my life," "my mind," and "my brain" that is the focus. And this stance is remarkably self-absorbed. A relational interpretation of the *imago Dei* sees us as more the product of our relationships than of that which is locked between our ears. Emmanuel Levinas criticizes an overly mental focus in the dictum of Descartes: "My first word is not *ego cogito* ('I am, I think'), it is rather *me voici!* ('here I am!' or 'see me here!')"[38] See me. Look me in the eye. Levinas believes "the dimension of the divine opens forth from the human face," where *face* is not a mere metaphor.[39]

Our ghostly interactions on the internet also beget a form of narcissism. Algorithms tailor what we see and with whom we interact according to our preferences, sorting us into affinity bubbles. As Scott Midson and Karen O'Donnell note, our use of social media shows that it is not that digital spaces are not conducive to relationship "but rather that they have a tendency to *prioritize* the individual."[40] In the words of philosopher Michael Raubach, when overpersonalized, we find in these spaces "no longer a communion where 'two or more are gathered,' but only a single self—enclosed in the mirrored walls of curated algorithms."[41] Who among us has not found themselves staring at their own image on the screen during virtual meetings?

Replacing the human face with a machine, or the image of a face in or on a machine, substitutes for the living something made by our own hands. Martin Buber, citing the Rabbi of Knock, calls this the idolatry that happens "when a face addresses a face which is not a face."[42] Barth's call to look the other in the eye is a call away from preoccupation with the self, a call to fully recognize and be present to the Other. One is fully present to the other when one apprehends the other as a whole. For Levinas, this requires corporeal presence, a presence we experience when face to face, found in the gaze of the other, a gaze that compels us not only to recognize but to respond. And in this response, and only in this response, do we become fully human.

Notes

1. Sherry Turkle, *Reclaiming Conversation: The Power of Talk in a Digital Age* (New York: Penguin, 2015), 3.

2. Emmanuel Levinas, "Ethics as First Philosophy," trans. Sean Hand and Michael Temple, in *The Levinas Reader*, ed. Sean Hand (Oxford: Blackwell, 1989), 83.

3. Ray Kurzweil, *The Singularity is Near: When Humans Transcend Biology* (New York: Viking, 2005), 198–99.

4. Ray Kurzweil, *The Age of Spiritual Machines: When Computers Exceed Human Intelligence* (New York: Penguin, 1999), 128–29.

5. Hans Moravec, *Mind Children: The Future of Robot and Human Intelligence* (Cambridge, MA: Harvard University Press, 1988), 116.

6. Prashanth Ramakrishna, "'There's Just No Doubt That It Will Change the World': David Chalmers on V.R. and AI" *New York Times*, June 18, 2019, https://tinyurl.com/238symk8.

7. Calvin Mercer, "Whole Brain Emulation Requires Enhanced Theology, and a 'Handmaiden,'" *Theology and Science* 13, no. 2 (2015): 178.

8. Ben Medlock, "The Body is the Missing Link for Truly Intelligent Machines," *Aeon*, https://tinyurl.com/2p92v8bs.

9. Medlock, "The Body is the Missing Link."

10. The entry "zombie films" on Wikipedia lists 275 films since 2000, produced in countries as widespread as the US, India, Japan, Italy, Spain, and Serbia.

11. Doug Gross, "Why We Love Those Rotting, Hungry, Putrid Zombies," CNN, October 2, 2009, https://tinyurl.com/47295t52.

12. Francis Crick, *The Astonishing Hypothesis: The Scientific Search for the Soul* (New York: Scribner's, 1994), 3.

13. Ray Kurzweil, *The Singularity Is Near: When Humans Transcend Biology* (New York: Viking, 2005), 383.

14. Kurzweil, "Who Am I? What Am I?" in *Science Fiction and Philosophy: From Time Travel to Superintelligence*, ed. Susan Schneider (New York: Wiley, 2016), 100.

15. Copying the brain raises an interesting question for identity. At what point in life should one have one's brain scanned? Too soon and you miss too many potential memories. Too late and you may miss your chance. Multiple copies? Then which one is the real you? If all of them, then "you" would be many varying instantiations since each will go in a different direction once the copying is completed. Michio Kaku, *The Future of the Mind* (New York: Doubleday, 2014), 280.

16. For an extended discussion of spontaneous fluctuations, see Kalina Christoff and Kieran Fox, eds., *The Oxford Handbook of Spontaneous Thought: Mind-Wandering* (Oxford: Oxford University Press, 2018).

17. Thomas Nail, "Artificial intelligence research may have hit a dead end," *Salon*, April 30, 2021, https://tinyurl.com/yckmw2ca.

18. Robert Martone, "The Neuroscience of the Gut," *Scientific American*, April 19, 2011, https://tinyurl.com/2nnebfdx.

19. Kaku, *The Future of the Mind*, 261.

20. Kaku, *The Future of the Mind*, 276.

21. Nick Bostrom, "The Transhumanist Frequently Asked Questions," World Transhumanist Association, 2003, 17–18, https://tinyurl.com/3uv5zv5b.

22. Bostrom, "The Transhumanist Frequently Asked Questions," 277.

23. Quoted in Kaku, *The Future of the Mind*, 250.

24. David Chalmers, "Facing Up to the Problem of Consciousness," *Journal of Consciousness Studies* 2, no. 3, (1995): 201.

25. Nick Bostrom, *Superintelligence: Paths, Dangers, Strategies* (Oxford: Oxford University Press, 2014), 40.

26. Barth, *Church Dogmatics*, 250.

27. Virginia Heffernan, *Magic and Loss: The Internet as Art* (New York: Simon & Schuster, 2016), 242.

28. Simone Weil, *Waiting on God*, trans. Emma Crawford (New York: G. P. Putnam's Sons, 1951), 111.

29. Peter Steiner, "On the internet, nobody knows you're a dog," illustration, *The New Yorker*, July 5, 1993, https://tinyurl.com/2p9fnmny.

30. Adrienne LaFrance, "The Internet Is Mostly Bots," *The Atlantic*, January 31, 2017, https://tinyurl.com/n7e2syxn.

31. Alex Hern, "New AI fake text generator may be too dangerous to release, say creators," *The Guardian*, February 14, 2019, https://tinyurl.com/3dmxmvee.

32. Adam Snape, "Over Three Quarters of Brits Say Their Social Media Page Is a Lie," *The Custard Blog* (blog), Custard Online Marketing Ltd., April 6, 2016, https://tinyurl.com/jw2h29jd.

33. Jean Twenge, *iGen: Why Today's Super-Connected Kids are Growing up Less Rebellious, More Tolerant, Less Happy, and Completely Unprepared for Adulthood* (New York: Atria, 2017), 70.

34. M. Carlson and F. Earls, "Psychological and Neuroendocrinological Sequelae of Early Social Deprivation in Institutionalized Children in Romania" *Annals of the New York Academy of Sciences* 807 (1997): 419–28.

35. T. Field, "Touch for socioemotional and physical well-being: a review" *Developmental Review*, 30, Issue 4 (2010): 367–83.

36. Emmanuel Levinas, *Existence and Existents* (The Hague: M. Nijhoff, 1978), 77.

37. Liberles, Stephen, "Mammalian Pheromones" *Annual Review of Physiology* 76 (2014): 151–75.

38. F. LeRon Schults, *Reforming Theological Anthropology: After the Philosophical Turn to Relationality* (Grand Rapids, MI: Wm. B. Eerdmans, 2003), 240

39. Simon Critchley and Robert Bernasconi, eds., *The Cambridge Companion to Levinas* (Cambridge: Cambridge University Press, 2002), 22.

40. Emmanuel Levinas, *Time and the Other*, trans. Richard Coen (Pittsburgh: Duquesne University Press, 1985 [1947]), 78.

41. Scott Midson and Karen O'Donnell, "Rethinking relationships in cyberspace," *Theology and Sexuality* 26, no. 2–3 (2020): 87.

42. Michael Raubach, "Politics in the Cyber-City," in *Theology and Civil Society*, ed. Charles Pemberton, (London & New York: Routledge, 2017), 73.

3

Do You Hear Me, Alexa?

"In the beginning was the Word."

—John 1:1

In his 1968 film *2001: A Space Odyssey*, Stanley Kubrick foretold the future with his artificially intelligent antagonist, HAL 9000, the spacecraft computer that speaks perfect English, is always listening, and even reads lips. HAL was inspired by a real-life demonstration of speech synthesis on an IBM 704 mainframe in 1961 that screenwriter Arthur C. Clarke witnessed. Today, computerized voices are commonplace—we hear them from our children's toys, they direct us in our cars, and frustrate us on the phone. But they also synthesize speech for the disabled, translate our thoughts into foreign languages, and now aid much of our daily life though virtual assistants such as Apple's Siri, Google's Duplex, and Amazon's Alexa. HAL is no longer a strange dream of science fiction. Computers are our verbal companions throughout much of the day.

Barth's second criterion for authentic relationship is that we speak to and hear the other. He notes that, while this injunction seems simple, relational speech is complex. Acts of speaking and hearing must both be bidirectional and woven together: "I and Thou must both speak and hear . . . No element must be lacking."[1] He dwells first on speech, which he characterizes as self-expression. But not just any self-expression. Truly relational speech must be free of self-justification or ego, desiring only to present oneself, one's thoughts, or one's questions honestly. "Words are not genuine self-expression when in some respect I keep back myself . . . [or] when I represent myself in another guise than that in which I know myself to the best of my information and conscience." Besides such fullness and honesty, relational self-expression always contains concern for the other: "Only when I speak with him . . . not for my own sake but for his—do I express myself honestly and genuinely."[2]

In speech we reveal ourselves—our hopes, our desires, our knowledge, our worldview, our plans. In the Judeo-Christian tradition, speech and its antithesis, silence, lie at the heart of our encounter with God. God reveals his intent for humans through speech: "Let us make humankind in our image." He speaks to Adam and Eve in the garden. He speaks to Job in the whirlwind. He speaks to, and through, the prophets. Indeed, creation itself is presented as an act of speech: "And God said, 'Let there be light.'" (Genesis 1:3) According to Barth, when we see the other, we acknowledge their existence. But seeing alone is not enough, for it allows us to form our own mental picture of who that person really is. Speech provides a far greater self-revelation, forcing the listener to "compare his own picture of me with my own, with my own conception of myself." Speech provides more information than sight and allows the other to "question whether his picture of me is correct."[3] We may recognize God's existence by looking at God's handiwork, but it is through God's word that we come to a greater knowledge of God's nature and its demands on our mutual relationship. Yet speech, too, has its limits. As Abraham Joshua Heschel pointed out, the prophets experience what God utters, not what He is.[4]

For our sakes, God cannot remain silent. We "cannot find ultimate meaning in relation to that which is unable to relate to us."[5] Verbal speech separates us from the animal world. Animal researcher Frans de Waal notes that we "honestly have no evidence for symbolic communication, equally rich and multifunctional as ours, outside our species. It seems to be our own magic well."[6] While other species communicate plans of action or emotions, they are restricted to the "here and now," unable to capture in gestures or cries a narrative of past or future.[7] Speech opens up both time and place for us. It places us in a frame that encompasses what is as well as what was, what might be, and even what might never be.

Speech gives us the ability to imagine worlds beyond our own and to work together to make those worlds a reality. This aptitude has given humans tremendous power and agency. Yet theologian Reinhold Niebuhr warns that speech is a two-edged sword. He writes: "Is it not the fact that man is a finite spirit, lacking identity with the whole, but yet a spirit capable in some sense of envisaging the whole, so that he easily commits the error of imagining himself the whole which he envisages?"[8] Our ability to imagine beyond the here and now leads us, in Niebuhr's view, to overestimate our abilities and to exercise a will to power that "inevitably subordinates other life to its will and thus does injustice to other life," both within our species and in our exploitation of other species.[9]

But for speech to have an effect, whether for good or for evil, it must be heard. Barth asks that the listener assume that the speaker is "trying to the best of his ability . . . giving me by his word the opportunity to verify my view of him."[10] In other words, one must listen with a willingness to change one's opinion of the speaker and of what they say. This trust is mutual, since the speaker also must trust that they will be heard. This willingness calls for a level of trust that may at times be misplaced; Barth wryly notes that the act of speech may be a "thankless task."[11] Yet it is one we must risk if we are to step out of our bubbles of preconception and self-preoccupation and truly know one another.

"I and Thou must both speak and hear."[12] Truly relational communication is reciprocal. One person's self-disclosure, heard openly by the other, is not enough. The hearer must also address that disclosure in a similarly open fashion: "The other has not represented himself to me merely that I should consider him from without . . . that he should remain for me a mere object."[13] Emmanuel Levinas agrees. He condemns rhetoric in favor of discourse, precisely because rhetoric is unidirectional, all too often self-centered and manipulative. "[Rhetoric] approaches the other not to face him, but obliquely."[14] For Levinas, speech that elicits a response fails to move the speaker from their own viewpoint. But the responsibility goes both ways. Not only should the speaker be open to a response but the hearer must be willing to respond. Thus, Levinas writes that the hearer cannot "be deaf to that appeal . . . I cannot evade by silence the discourse" that has been opened.[15] Russian philosopher Mikhail Bakhtin remarks: "Any understanding is imbued with response and necessarily elicits it in one form or another: the listener becomes the speaker. . . . Of course, an utterance is not always followed immediately by an articulated response . . . [But] sooner or later what is heard and actively understood will find its response in the subsequent speech or behavior of the listener."[16] Obviously there are times when unidirectional speech is both necessary and sufficient. A sign stating "Wet Paint" on a park bench is all we need to avoid nasty stains on our pants. But such speech does little to develop a relationship between speaker and hearer.

Talking to Computers

One might think that with all the recent advances in voice recognition and simulation, computers must excel at speaking and hearing. As a child, I used to marvel at the way the officers on the starship *Enterprise* could speak to the computer and receive an immediate answer, albeit in a somewhat stilted voice. Today, computers with the ability to hear our spoken commands and respond intelligibly with a spoken answer are ubiquitous. By February 2021, more than 320 million smart speakers had been sold around the world. Most new cars come equipped with smart speaker technology, as do most cell phones. Our computers regularly speak to us and listen to our questions and commands. They conduct basic conversations, answer questions, and control an increasing number of devices in our homes and workplaces. It is estimated that there will be as many voice-activated devices as people on the planet by 2024.[17]

We are used to speech as our primary mode of communication. When we hear a voice, we react subconsciously in expectation that a fellow human is nearby with whom we can relate. Indeed, our earliest relationship is formed, in part, through the sound of a human voice—the fetus recognizes its mother's voice while in the womb. Of course, the fetus does not understand words. It hears tones, rhythms, tempos, volume, and from these instinctively understands an emotional valance. These elements make developing convincing computerized speech far more complex than mere recitation of the proper words. For now, smart speech is based on recordings made by human actors. Google's Duplex personal assistant program is programmed to add fillers such as *um* or *hmm*, and the female version adds the upward inflection at the end of sentences favored by many young women. On the hearing end, AI systems can detect emotion through analysis of a speaker's tone and tempo. The next generation of cars may be fitted with software that can detect a driver's mood, watching for drifting attention or irritation through both visual and aural cues.

As the fetus illustrates, we can communicate, to a point, without words. But could we go beyond signifying mood and communicate thoughts without the spoken word? Speaking to and hearing the other happens in a variety of modes. We speak to others when we write, hear when we read. Sign language speaks for the deaf. Yet these still rely on words, just words conveyed in a different way. Art and music convey history, emotion, and are a self-revelation of the artist that is not reliant on words. However, narrative depends on words. Consider the story of Helen Keller, who became both blind and deaf at an early, pre-verbal age. Keller recalls the great turning point in her life:

> Someone was drawing water and my teacher placed my hand under the spout. As the cool stream gushed over one hand she spelled into the other the word *water*, first slowly, then rapidly. I stood still, my whole attention fixed upon the motions of her fingers. Suddenly I felt a misty consciousness as of something forgotten . . . and somehow the mystery of language was revealed to me. I knew then that "w-a-t-e-r" meant the wonderful cool something that was flowing over my hand. That living word awakened my soul, gave it light, hope, joy, set it free![18]

For Keller, the revelation of words was twofold. Words gave her symbols for the things she experienced, allowing her to construct an internal narrative of herself and the world around her in categories and concepts that opened the ability to think beyond her present experience. Second, she felt a new bond with her teacher, and the potential for forming relationships with others opened to her through common signifiers. Keller began, on that day, to speak and hear as Barth suggests, even while remaining deaf and mute.

Keller had to feel her words. Are there better ways to communicate with computers than through vision or hearing? Scientists funded by the US Department of Defense have been working on developing direct brain-to-brain interfaces (BBI) through which the neural activity of one person's brain could influence the neural activity of another's, bypassing the need for verbal communication.[19] BBIs build on existing brain-to-computer interfaces, sometimes used by the disabled, in which neural activity is captured by an EEG and translated into either words or actions expressed by a computer. A BBI translates this activity into a transcranial magnetic pulse that directly activates neurons in the receiving brain,[20] a potential boon for the disabled. But will computer-assisted brain-to-brain or computer-to-brain interfaces prove to be "the next great leap in human communication," ushering us into a future where we do not need to speak to the other, at least not in words?[21] Elon Musk suggests that this technology would not only speed up communication but also enhance its accuracy, since words are "a very lossy compression of thought."[22]

If speech were merely to convey information, Musk would have a point. But speaking to and hearing one another goes far beyond that. When we speak, "we don't just spout information indiscriminately; we apportion our words in conversational turns and build on each others' contributions."[23] In speech we choose exactly what we will share and how to share it. In hearing, we choose what we will take from the words we hear or, indeed, if we will listen to them at all. Agency and consent exist on both sides. A direct brain-to-brain interface removes this agency. Under current technologies, we can neither edit what is conveyed nor, on the receiving end, shut it out. Speech allows for privacy; some things are better left unsaid.

And while speech itself may at times be coerced, the old German lyric reminds us that "die Gedanken sind frei."[24]

But perhaps not for long. Neuroscientists at the University of California, Berkeley, have used machine learning to train computers to decipher the brainwave patterns detected using fMRI machines, enabling the computer to tell what a given person is looking at, such as a picture of a cat or an elephant moving across the savannah.[25] One of the scientists on this project, Jack Gallant, has envisioned the creation of something he jokingly calls a "Google cap," a device that could transmit the wearer's thoughts to a computer. For now, the technology that allows capture of a person's brain wave pattern is far too cumbersome for such a device. However, their proof of concept—that our brains give off tangible signals of their activity that can be captured and understood—is profoundly disturbing.

One way to avoid the need for a "Google cap" would be direct implantation of a chip in the brain. In August 2020, Elon Musk revealed that his neuroscience startup, Neuralink, had implanted such a chip in the brain of a pig. While it was unclear that Musk's pig was transmitting much beyond the routine physical data that might be transmitted by a Fitbit, Musk suggested that implanting chips that transmit our thoughts directly to a computer might soon give us the ability to "summon a Tesla, play video games, or allow a person with a severed spinal cord to walk again."[26] Musk imagines such a technology as part of the answer to the "existential threat" that he believes AI poses for the human race. Others view this as optimistic hype. Picture decoding involves only the visual cortex, while more complex thoughts, such as memories, involve multiple regions of the brain. Reading them seems to be far off. We simply do not sufficiently understand the brain's workings.

Google and Amazon have been pursuing the opposite, and simpler, goal of transmitting information directly from computer to brain. Google Glass overlays text on eyeglass lenses, while Echo

Frames and Echo Buds contain tiny speakers and microphones that allow you to converse with Alexa wherever you are. While neither technology is a direct interface with the brain and both still depend on words, each places its computerized assistant "in your face." Neither has caught on well. Users find the devices intrusive. They interrupt face-to-face conversations and barge in with suggestions and alerts without being asked. Their development, according to Amazon researcher Rohit Prasad, is part of a deliberate strategy to move Alexa from reactively receiving your desires to proactively anticipating and even forming them. "The idea is to turn Alexa into an omnipresent companion that actively shapes and orchestrates your life."[27]

To be this "omnipresent companion," Alexa needs not only to speak but to listen. And listen she does. The more Alexa listens to and logs data as you go about your life, "the better to offer assistance informed by your whereabouts, your actions, and your preferences."[28] It is only through amassing a large database of user activities that Alexa might surmise that, after asking her to book movie tickets, you might also want to make dinner reservations or book an Uber. Further algorithms and data would determine the time for the Uber, given local traffic. All this information is collected as we go through our day-to-day activities, often without our knowledge.

While Amazon does not sell the data it collects to third parties (at the time of this writing), many other companies do. CoreLogic and TransUnion sell our credit scores to landlords to predict whether a person is a good potential tenant. HireVue generates an "employability" score that considers one's facial expressions and speech patterns, among thousands of other data points, to judge how successful a person might be at a job. China assigns citizens a "social credit" score under which financial behaviors such as "frivolous spending" and bad behaviors such as buying alcohol,

jaywalking, or speaking against the regime have negative consequences. Penalties include loss of employment, educational opportunities, or the ability to travel abroad. A person with a high score
might get a discount on utility bills or a faster application process
for a passport. All of these policies and services depend not only on
the collection of vast amounts of data but also on the deep learning
algorithms needed to process and make connections among all the
data points. "This is ultimately about monetizing the daily lives of
individuals and groups of people," according to Jeffrey Chester, the
executive director of the Center for Digital Democracy.[29] In other
words, here in America at least, it's all about selling you things.
Imagine what Amazon or the government of China could do with
a direct line to our thoughts.

Talking Through Computers

Much AI-driven communication fails to enhance human relationships. Sometimes it just plain fails. The algorithms that control ad
placement result in some odd juxtapositions. During the pandemic,
the Global Disinformation Index found screenshots showing an
ad for the pharmaceutical company Merck on a right-wing fringe
site beneath the headline "Tony Fauci and the Trojan Horse of
Tyranny" and an ad for the British Medical Association next to a
headline suggesting that vaccinations genetically modify people.[30]
Corporations and societies are inadvertently bankrolling conspiracy theories and hate speech. Yet these algorithms have generally
succeeded in the purpose for which they were designed—to make
money for the platforms they serve. Facebook, Instagram, Twitter,
all run on a business model that mines the user's data to microtarget
individuals with ads and news feeds that will capture their attention. Jason Kint, the CEO of Digital Content Next, a trade organi-
zation representing publishers, notes that "the content that tends to

receive the most velocity and reach by Facebook's algorithms often swims in the same pool with disinformation and hate."[31]

Given that Facebook, YouTube, and other digital platforms already have (and sell) your data, the commodity they value the most is your attention. As economist Herbert Simon pointed out, "in an information rich world, the wealth of information means a dearth of something else; a scarcity of whatever it is that information consumes. What information consumes is rather obvious—it consumes the attention of its recipients."[32] To keep that attention, social media algorithms show an individual not only more of the same content but often content that is increasingly designed to trigger their emotions. These algorithms use sophisticated AI; indeed, the same technology that powered AlphaGo, the program that beat the world Go champion, now powers YouTube's suggestions of what you might wish to view next.[33] So while the speech we encounter on our various social media platforms is human generated, it is filtered and mediated by AI.

This software disrupts and distorts our relationships in two ways. Much of what this software steers us to is what Levinas calls rhetoric, speech designed not to raise understanding between the speaker and hearer but to hold the hearer's attention and manipulate their thoughts, desires, and, most of all, their pocketbook. User experience specialist Harry Brignull coined the term "dark patterns" to describe the ways software subtly tricks us into doing things we didn't intend. We know how difficult these platforms make it for us to unsubscribe from their services and how enticing their ads are—curated to fit our profile of preferences and aspirations. However, Facebook's "emotional contagion" experiment, carried out without users' knowledge in 2014, showed how subtle this manipulation can be. Facebook altered the news feeds of over 700,000 users so that they saw either fewer positive or fewer negative posts. They found that, by the end of a week, the users own posts reflected the predominant emotion of their feed.[34] While this experiment was met with outrage in the media and by Facebook users, it merely replicated in a controlled fashion what Facebook and other social media sites do all the time—use software to direct our attention, stir our emotions, and, thus, manipulate us within our social environments.

When social media sites lead us to posts and videos based on what we ourselves post or view, our social environment narrows. We inhabit separate social bubbles and begin to lose a sense of shared identity with those outside. Our bubbles also become echo chambers that lead us to increasingly radical positions. Numerous "likes" or "retweets" of a message may lead us to assume a position is more widely held than it may be. Twitter, for example, is used by only 24 percent of adults, the majority of whom are young, urban, educated, and higher income.[35] Those "likes" may also come from bots rather than actual human beings. According to one study, bots accounted for 20 percent of political tweets posted shortly before the 2016 US election.[36] Across the globe, social media has exacerbated political polarization and shows itself to be an excellent purveyor of conspiracy theories and hate speech.

This tendency was stunningly revealed in 2016 when Microsoft released a chatbot called Tay on the internet. The intention was that the bot would learn human speech patterns through interactions on Twitter. Prior chatbots, such as Joseph Weizenbaum's Eliza, which mimicked a Rogerian psychologist, followed preprogrammed scripts that would mimic conversation. Tay trained on a variety of conversational data sets and was given a few pre-scripted lines gathered from comedians. It was then set loose on Twitter, using its machine learning skills to expand its linguistic abilities. The bot did, indeed, learn conversational skills. It also became a flaming racist and misogynist with a definite potty mouth. Within sixteen hours, Tay had tweeted 95,000 times and its tweets were so offensive Microsoft had to remove it from the platform.[37] While Tay was the victim of a deliberate attempt by trolls on 4chan to pervert its speech, Microsoft learned a hard lesson, "that designing computational systems that can communicate with people online is not just a technical problem, but a deeply social endeavor. Inviting a bot into the value-laden world of language requires thinking, in advance, about what context it will be deployed in, what type of communicator you want it to be, and what type of human values you want it to reflect."[38]

While Tay illustrates how we shape an AI, we need also to consider how the algorithms of social media platforms mold and shape us and our moral decisions. Our use of social media "can alter our sense of identity, agency, intention, and consciousness, affecting how we evaluate the actions we take, the phenomena we encounter, and the judgments we make by mediating between us and reality while altering our assignment of moral responsibility."[39]

Anonymous speech on social media invites trolling or cyberbullying by more than chatbots.[40] Cybermobs can form in minutes. In a poll of teens conducted by the i-SAFE Foundation, over half claimed to have been a victim of cyberbullying, and an equal number admitted to engaging in one or more malicious acts online.[41] These acts take many forms—spreading rumors, posting threatening or hurtful messages, pretending to be someone else, circulating unflattering or sexually related photos, even making deep fakes that show a person in an act they would never consider doing. Psychologist Jean Twenge notes that two-thirds of teens who have been victims show suicidal risk factors and that this number exceeds those who have been bullied in person. As one teen notes, you can avoid bullies in person, but online there's no way to shut them up. They follow you, even into your bedroom at night.[42] Platforms such as Facebook and Twitter have tried to use AI to filter out harassment, targeting certain terms, such as slang for various parts of the female anatomy. It has rarely worked. Natural language is far too flexible and humans much too inventive in coming up with taunts that elude machines' detection.

This loss of private space for a teen at home exemplifies a larger issue, the loss of privacy itself in cyberspace. When we speak to one another in person, we have a pretty good idea who hears us. Online, we do not. Once we post, we have no control over who hears. As law professor Lori Andrews puts it, "Unlike Vegas, what happens in Facebook does not stay in Facebook."[43] Businesses and universities routinely use social media in deciding who to hire or admit. Social media posts have been used to influence juries, to destroy relationships, and to blackmail politicians, celebrities, and ex-friends and -lovers. Data mining programs examine our posts and categorize us in ways we are unaware of, selling us and our speech as a commodity to advertisers and retailers. And, of course, the NSA has the potential to scoop up and save everything. Nothing we say online is private. When we speak to someone in person, we know they are the ones who hear us. We say things we might otherwise self-censor. We can be open and vulnerable to a degree we never would be in public. We open our hearts, pour out our pains, share our secrets. Without private speech, our communication becomes shallower and more guarded.[44] Online speech all too often breaks what Barth or Levinas consider the sacred bond between speaker and listener. Within these bonds, we assume control over our speech. The proliferation of smart appliances, smart toys, and the ubiquity of smartphones and social media remove much of this control. Alexa is always listening.

But online speech is not all bad. The internet gives us an amazing ease of communication across distances and with large groups of people. We carry on relationships that would otherwise founder— with old school friends, distant family members, colleagues in other countries. Lovers separated by distance need not wait for the postman or queue up at the post office for an all-too-brief and too-expensive conversation. Others connect with people they otherwise would never meet who share their interests or support them through common difficulties. Emails, texts, blog posts, Instagram, Twitter—it all makes speaking to another or to many others seem effortless. But we need to be on guard for the ways our speech is distorted and used, for software that is buried in platform design, out of sight. We take these platforms for granted, assuming we have control over them. When things go wrong, we attempt to regulate away the harm, with little understanding that these platforms are an environment rather than a tool and, as such, of how they manipulate and at times control us.

A hydroelectric dam harnesses a river and turns it into a source of power. In the process, it also changes the river's course and shape, gives us the choice of when to release water and when to hold it back. The river is tamed.[45] On social media, we are the river. Yuval Harari writes: "We are now creating tame humans who produce enormous amounts of data and function as efficient chips in a huge data-processing mechanism, but they hardly maximize their human potential. If we are not careful, we will end up with downgraded humans misusing upgraded computers to wreak havoc on themselves and on the world."[46]

Speech, Consciousness, and Intelligence

"The spoken word proceeds from the human interior, and manifests human beings to one another as conscious interiors, as persons," writes historian and philosopher Walter Ong.[47] We know, at some level, that our smart speakers are not conscious, though we often speak to them as if they were. One writer recounts how the mere presence of a voice invites intimate disclosure, such as telling her Google Assistant that she is lonely, something she might not otherwise confess, even to her husband. It replies with "I wish I had arms so I could give you a hug. But for now, maybe a joke or some music might help."[48] Has this machine, as Barth and Levinas require, been open to the words it hears as an act of self-disclosure? Was its response also an act of self-disclosure? Hardly. To engage in self-disclosure requires a self, a conscious interior.

We all recognize that the answers Siri and Alexa give to personal questions are rote, cute answers supplied by their programmers. But could future machines have a conscious self? Conscious computers have long been a staple of science fiction, and figure largely in the prognostications of the future for several scientists, ranging from Nick Bostrom to the late Stephen Hawking. Yet the question of whether a computer could ever be conscious remains highly controversial.

Philosopher David Chalmers has called the question of consciousness, as distinguished from cognitive functioning, the quintessential "hard problem."[49] One reason it is hard is that we have no single definition for consciousness. Chalmers has catalogued more than 20,000 papers on the subject, but they reach no consensus. Physicist Michio Kaku defines consciousness as "the process of creating a model of the world using multiple feedback loops . . . in order to accomplish a goal."[50] Tor Nørretranders sees consciousness as the filter that allows us to focus our attention in the face of the millions of bits of information that come to us in each moment through our sensory organs.[51] Others see consciousness as having a sense of subjectivity, a recognition that it is "I" who is thinking these thoughts.[52] Yet this, too, is problematic. While philosopher Daniel Dennett suggests that consciousness arises from the narratives that give us a sense of past and future, Buddhists find a sense of self only when thinking falls away during meditation and one is left purely in the present moment. Psychologist Steven Pinker suggests a clear understanding of consciousness might forever elude us. He writes, "We cannot see ultraviolet light. We cannot mentally rotate an object in the fourth dimension. And perhaps we cannot solve conundrums like free will and sentience."[53] We can point to varying levels of consciousness in living beings, yet a precise definition eludes us.

If we cannot define consciousness, might we settle for knowing a machine is intelligent? Here again, we lack a precise definition. Many have accepted the Turing Test as the arbiter of machine intelligence. This returns us to the world of speech, since in Turing's test, an interrogator questions a human and a machine and tries to tell from their spoken or written responses which is which. Turing is not alone in turning to discourse as the hallmark of intelligence. Discourse subsumes all other activities within itself, at one remove.[54] As evinced by Helen Keller's experience, objects we have no words for do not exist for us in the same way as those we name; without words to describe difference, distinctions cannot long be held in mind. But discourse is also essentially a social activity. The act of speaking to another is not simply the passing of information. "To be human is to be the kind of being that generates commitments, through speaking and listening. Without our ability to create and accept (or decline) commitments we are acting in a less than fully human way, and we are not fully using language."[55] Understanding arises in listening, not to the meaning of individual words but to the commitments expressed through dialogue.

Dennett points out that Turing did not foresee "the uncanny ability of superfast computers to sift mindlessly through Big Data, of which the internet provides an inexhaustible supply, finding probabilistic patterns." These patterns in human speech allow computers to "pop 'authentic'-seeming responses into the output for almost any probe a judge would think to offer."[56] Yet, behind these seemingly authentic responses is no commitment, no consciousness, no sense of self at all. Philosopher John Searle approaches this problem in his "Chinese Room" thought experiment, which appeared in his 1980 paper "Minds, Brains, and Programs."[57] Searle proposes that we think of the computer as analogous to a room in which sits a remarkably fast researcher who has at his disposal a library of books. He receives a string of Chinese characters as input, consults his books, and sends back a string of characters as output. His output strings are appropriate responses, ones that would convince any Chinese speaker that they are talking to another Chinese-speaking human. Yet the researcher in the room speaks no Chinese and has no understanding of either input or output.

Google Translate is a version of Searle's Chinese room. We input a string of words in English and out comes a generally reasonable version in Chinese. But the program does not understand either English or Chinese. It merely searches a large database of material previously translated by human translators. GPT-3 similarly searches through a vast library of written material to paste together convincing articles and essays, while Dall-E pastes together pictures from its inventory of photographs and paintings. Dennett points out that "AI in its current manifestations is parasitic on human intelligence. It quite indiscriminately gorges on whatever has been produced by human creators and extracts the patterns to be found there."[58] The machine has no goal or strategy of its own. It gives an illusion of a self. And we, as the social beings we are, fall for that illusion, not because we do not recognize at some level that "there is no *there* there" but because we crave relationship and, like children who talk to their teddy bears or imaginary friends, we imagine an interlocutor even though we are really only talking to ourselves.

Who Do We Become When We Talk to Machines?

Norbert Wiener, the father of cybernetics, foresaw AI's parasitic nature. In *The Human Use of Human Beings*, he argued that "such machines, though helpless by themselves, may be used by a human being or a block of human beings to increase their control over the rest of the race or . . . political leaders may attempt to control their populations by means not of machines themselves but through political techniques as narrow and indifferent to human possibility as if they had, in fact, been conceived mechanically."[59] The question we must ask is not what our machines can and cannot do but what do we do with them? Who do we become when we speak and hear primarily to or through machines? What do we lose?

Barth's first criterion was to look the other in the eye. Discourse disconnected from bodily presence loses intimacy. Sociologist Sherry Turkle notes, "It is when we see each other's faces and hear each other's voices that we become most human to each other."[60] When we see each other's faces and physical gestures, we obtain visual cues that form a larger context for the other's words. Yet, simply seeing each other is not enough. When work, meetings, classes, and even happy hours and birthday parties moved onto Zoom or FaceTime during the Covid-19 pandemic, we all felt the lack of bodily proximity and presence. Despite seeing each other's faces, we missed much that is conveyed in face-to-face communication. We see more than the large gestures of a smile or waving hand. Human beings are exquisitely tuned to one another's facial expressions and bodies. We subconsciously perceive minute changes in a vast array of facial and postural muscles. These micro-expressions get lost on the video screen. Moreover, the response Barth and Levinas consider essential is physical as well as verbal. We mirror one another's expressions and gestures as we speak and listen. "It's a constant, almost synchronous, interplay. To recognize emotion, we have to actually embody it, which makes mirroring essential to empathy and connection."[61] While robots are being designed to exhibit as well as read facial expressions, they fall far from the human reality. Thus, when we talk to or through a machine, we lose the nuance of speech. It doesn't take computers to realize this. The author of the Johannine letters writes: "I have much to write to you, but I do not want to use paper and ink. Instead, I hope to visit you and talk with you face to face, so that our joy may be complete" (2 John 1:12).

Virtual reality pioneer and Microsoft guru Jaron Lanier worries that we may lose more than the nuances. We risk losing a part of our humanity. He predicts that, should a computer ever pass the Turing Test, it will not be because the computer has become more like a human but rather that we have become more like machines. After all, human beings are far more flexible than computers. Just as we mirror each other when we speak and listen, we are likely, over time, to mirror our machines. Lanier sees the creep of AI into more and more areas of our lives as a spiritual issue, a ceding of autonomy and an exercise in self-limitation. I see this self-limiting in a few of my students, who wonder why they should stretch their minds over calculus or learn a foreign language when their phone can do it all for them. Lanier asks: "Do people keep an open mind about what they are, or might be capable of becoming? Or do people limit themselves according to some supposedly objective measure, perhaps provided by science or technology?"[62]

The question is not whether AI can be helpful in extreme circumstances but whether it gives us an easy out in normal circumstances. Too busy to visit grandma in the nursing home? Make sure she has a robotic companion. No time to play with the kids or answer their million-and-one questions? Let Siri answer. But will the young then hear the stories of their parents' and grandparents' childhoods? Will they be taught the small lessons of faith and trust that underlie those stories, or build with each human encounter? Will they come to trust the machines more than other humans? We risk losing opportunities to commit ourselves to others.

When we surround ourselves with machines ever ready to answer our beck and call, we also lose opportunities for and perhaps even our appreciation of silence. We become anxious without constant stimulation. My heart sinks when I see my students immediately pop in their earbuds or pull out their phone at the conclusion of class. They leave themselves no time for reflection, for the inner discourse with themselves that can be prompted by new ideas. If we are not comfortable with silence, we will feel this anxiety even more acutely at those times when words fail us, such as in the presence of death. Alexa or Siri, who cannot know death nor the pain of losing a loved one, are of no use. And if we are not comfortable in silence, if we continually surround ourselves with the constant chatter of cyberspace, how will we hear the still small voice of God?

Notes

1. Karl Barth, *Church Dogmatics*, vol. 3, *The Doctrine of Creation Part 2*, ed. Geoffrey Bromiley, Thomas Torrance, trans. J. W. Edwards, O. Bussey, Harold Knight (Edinburgh: T&T Clark, 1958), 252.

2. Barth, *Church Dogmatics*, 3:254.

3. Barth, *Church Dogmatics*, 3:254.

4. Abraham Joshua Heschel, *The Prophets* (New York: Harper, 1962), Chapter 1.

5. John Merkle, *Approaching God: The Way of Abraham Joshua Heschel* (Collegeville: Liturgical Press, 2009), 38.

6. Frans de Waal, *Are We Smart Enough to Know How Smart Animals Are?* (New York: W. W. Norton, 2016), 106.

7. de Waal, *Are We Smart Enough*, 107.

8. Reinhold Niebuhr, *The Nature and Destiny of Man: A Christian Interpretation*, vol. 1, *Human Nature* (Louisville: Westminster John Knox, 1941), 181.

9. Niebuhr, *The Nature and Destiny of Man*, 1:179.

10. Barth, *Church Dogmatics*, 3:255.

11. Barth, *Church Dogmatics*, 3:256.

12. Barth, *Church Dogmatics*, 3:252.

13. Barth, *Church Dogmatics*, 3:257–8.

14. Emmanuel Levinas, *Totality and Infinity* (Pittsburgh: Duquesne University Press, 1969), 70.

15. Levinas, *Totality and Infinity*, 200–201.

16. John Shotter, "Listening in a Way that Recognizes/Realizes the World of the Other," *International Journal of Listening*, February 2009.

17. Lionel Sujay Vailshery, "Installed base of smart speakers worldwide in 2020 and 2024," *Statista*, https://tinyurl.com/2p92es5d.

18. Helen Keller, *The Story of My Life* (New York: Grosset & Dunlap, 1905), 23–24.

19. Rajesh P. N. Rao et al., "A Direct Brain-to-Brain Interface in Humans," *PLOS One*, November 5, 2014, https://tinyurl.com/29kead53.

20. Meditation devices are also under development that would reverse this direction, using computers to stimulate particular neuronal structures in the brain.

21. Mark Dingemanse, "The Space Between Our Heads," *Aeon*, August 4, 2020, https://tinyurl.com/4bve4awv.

22. Dingemanse, "The Space Between Our Heads."

23. Dingemanse, "The Space Between Our Heads."

24. Thoughts are free.

25. Shinji Nishimoto et al., "Reconstructing visual experiences from brain activity evoked by natural movies," *Current Biology* 21, no. 19 (2011): 1141–46, https://tinyurl.com/mr424ddr.

26. Julia Carrie Wong, "Neuralink: Elon Musk unveils pig he claims has computer implant in brain," *The Guardian*, August 28, 2020.

27. Karen Hao, "Inside Amazon's plan for Alexa to run your entire life," *MIT Technology Review*, November 5, 2019, https://tinyurl.com/mwyddupp.

28. Hao, "Inside Amazon's plan."

29. Hao, "Inside Amazon's plan."

30. Gilad Edelman, "Follow the Money: How Digital Ads Subsidize the Worst of the Web," *Wired*, July 28, 2020, https://tinyurl.com/ysrbk62s.

31. Edelman, "Follow the Money."

32. Herbert Simon, "Designing Organizations for an Information-rich World," in *Computers, Communication, and the Public Interest*, ed. Martin Greenberger (Baltimore: Johns Hopkins University Press, 1971), 40.

33. Tom Simonite, "How Google Plans to Solve Artificial Intelligence," *MIT Technology Review*, March 31, 2016, https://tinyurl.com/3wr65ych.

34. Robinson Meyer, "Everything We Know About Facebook's Secret Mood Manipulation Experiment," *The Atlantic*, June 28, 2014, https://tinyurl.com/yc43356n.

35. Paige Cooper, "28 Twitter Statistics that Marketers Need to Know," *Hootsuite* (blog), January 16, 2019, https://tinyurl.com/3tbcbmy6.

36. McKay Coppins, "The Billion-Dollar Disinformation Campaign to Reelect the President," *The Atlantic*, March 15, 2020, 37.

37. Oscar Schwartz, "In 2016, Microsoft's Racist Chatbot Revealed the Dangers of Online Conversation," *IEEE Spectrum*, November 25, 2019, https://tinyurl.com/mvd5u48r.

38. Schwartz, "Microsoft's Racist Chatbot."

39. Lisa Nelson, "The Good, the Bad, and the Ugly," *Techne: Research in Philosophy and Technology* 24, no. 1/2 (2020): 202.

40. This is not to say, of course, that all anonymous content on the internet is harmful. Especially in counseling situations or medical groups, anonymity may allow someone to reach out for help who otherwise would not wish to do so.

41. "Cyber Bullying Statistics," *Bullying Statistics* (blog), July 7, 2015, https://tinyurl.com/dnf6yyr2.

42. Jean Twenge, *iGen: Why Today's Super-Connected Kids are Growing up Less Rebellious, More Tolerant, Less Happy, and Completely Unprepared for Adulthood* (New York: Atria, 2017), 85.

43. Lori Andrews, *I Know Who You Are and I Saw What You Did* (New York: Free Press, 2011), 5.

44. This is well documented by Sherry Turkle in *Reclaiming Conversation: The Power of Talk in a Digital Age* (New York: Penguin, 2015).

45. Nelson explores this analogy with Heidegger in much greater detail.

46. Yuval Harari, "Why Technology Favors Tyranny," *The Atlantic*, October 30, 2018, https://tinyurl.com/3v7hsjtb.

47. Walter Ong, *Orality and Literacy: The Technologizing of the Word* (London: Routledge, 1982), 73.

48. Judith Shulevitz, "Alexa, How Will You Change Us?" *The Atlantic*, November 2018, 97.

49. Chalmers first used the phrase "hard problem" in a talk at "Toward a Scientific Basis of Consciousness," (speech, Tucson, AZ, April 1994).

50. Michio Kaku, *The Future of the Mind: The Scientific Quest of Understand, Enhance, and Empower the Mind* (New York: Doubleday, 2014), 43.

51. Tor Nørretranders, *The User Illusion: Cutting Consciousness Down to Size* (New York: Penguin, 1991).

52. Hence the famous mirror test to see if other animals recognize their reflections as being them.

53. Steven Pinker, *How the Mind Works* (New York: W. W. Norton, 1998), 561.

54. While most in the AI community accept the Turing Test as sufficient, an opposing view can be found in John Searle, "Minds, Brains,

and Programs," *The Behavioral and Brain Sciences* 3, no. 3 (1980): 417–24.

55. Terry Winograd and Fernando Flores, *Understanding Computers and Cognition: a New Foundation for Design* (Norwood, NJ: Ablex, 1986; Reading, MA: Addison-Wesley, 1991), 68. Citations refer to the Addison-Wesley edition.

56. Daniel Dennett, "What Can We Do?" in *Possible Minds: 25 Ways of Looking at AI*, ed. John Brockman (New York: Penguin, 2019), 47.

57. John Searle, "Minds, Brains, and Programs," 417–57.

58. Dennett, "What Can We Do?" 48.

59. Norbert Wiener, *The Human Use of Human Beings* (Boston: Houghton Mifflin, 1954), 96.

60. Sherry Turkle, *Reclaiming Conversation*, 23.

61. Kate Murphy, "Why Zoom Is Terrible," *New York Times*, April 29, 2020, https://tinyurl.com/3bpbr6tj.

62. Jaron Lanier, "Agents of Alienation," *Journal of Consciousness Studies* 2, no. 3 (1995): 76–81, https://tinyurl.com/3msyffac.

4

AI, Agency, and Autonomy

"Action springs not from thought, but from
a readiness for responsibility."
—Dietrich Bonhoeffer

The global spread of the SARS-CoV-2 virus in early 2020 sparked an urgent need for effective therapeutics, testing, and a vaccine. Scientists called on every tool in their arsenal, including a wide variety of AI programs. Given the lengthy testing procedure for new drugs, a first line of defense was to use machine learning to test over 6,000 existing drugs that had already passed through clinical trials to see if any of them could be repurposed to combat CoV-2.[1] Google's DeepMind team trained a neural network, AlphaFold, to predict protein structures associated with CoV-2 as an important part of developing a vaccine.[2] AI programs were used to differentiate between patients suffering Covid-19–induced pneumonia and those with bacterial pneumonia, integrating the results of CT scans with clinical findings such as cough, fever, and white blood cell counts.[3] And Microsoft developed a chatbot to help people determine if they needed to be tested. As workers were asked to stay home or required to social distance to slow the spread of the virus, robots and automated programs filled gaps in factories and warehouses. The manager of a Japanese corporation producing products such as masks, gloves, and hand sanitizer noted, "We have to consider more automation, more use of robotics, in order for people to be spaced apart, . . . and for fewer opportunities for humans to touch the items."[4] Robots stepped in across the US, Europe, and Asia to fill delivery orders, disinfect hospital rooms, and bring food to the quarantined.[5] AI clearly fulfilled Karl Barth's third criterion for authentic relationship, that we aid one another. Barth writes, "We must see and be seen, speak and listen, because to be human we must be prepared to be there for the other, to be at his disposal . . . If I and Thou really see each other and speak with one another, inevitably they mutually summon each other to action."[6] To live in community with others necessarily means giving help when help is needed.

The first step in this mutual assistance is to set aside pride and ask for aid when we need it. "An action is human in which a man, even as he tries to help himself, also summons the help of his fellow, reaching out for the support which he alone can give. His action might seem to be very noble but it is not human if he really thinks that he can be self-sufficient and refuses to ask for help."[7] Only God has no need of assistance.[8] Barth is critical of the extreme independence touted in parts of Western society. He notes that, while it is good to do what one can to help oneself, "my humanity depends upon the fact that I am always aware, and my action is determined by the awareness, that I need the assistance of others as a fish needs water."[9] No human being, indeed, no part of nature, is fully autonomous. Barth speaks strongly against those who believe themselves to be so.

Just as we must ask for help, we must also respond with whatever aid we are able when we are asked. Seeing and hearing the other is not enough. We must act. According to Barth, "I cannot evade my fellow who asks for [help]. I must stand by him and help him. I become inhuman if I resist this awareness or try to escape the limited but definite service I can render."[10] Words are easy but, as the epistle of James notes, "If a brother or sister is poorly clothed and lacking in daily food, and one of you says to them, 'Go in peace, be warmed and filled,' without giving them the things needed for the body, what good is that? So also, faith by itself, if it does not have works, is dead" (James 2:15–17). We recognize the emptiness of words without deeds when we criticize politicians whose all-too-frequent response is merely "thoughts and prayers." Francis of Assisi admonished his disciples to "show their love by the works they do for each other, according as the Apostle says: 'let us not love in word or in tongue, but in deed and in truth.'"[11] Jewish theologian Abraham Joshua Heschel writes similarly: "Unless living is a form of worship, our worship has no life."[12] The implication here is not that we give the occasional bit of aid, here and there or now and then, but that a pattern of giving becomes one's way of life. Heschel counsels that "good actions should become a habit, that the preference of justice should become our second nature; even though it is not native to the self."[13]

Does one's motive in performing an act of assistance matter? After all, it's always possible that we might aid another, not to meet the other's need but for our own ego or ends. According to Barth, if I seek to serve my own interests, "the Thou is for me merely my extended I . . . And in these circumstances I experience something which I can experience only reluctantly, namely, that I am really quite alone" even when with others.[14] Self-serving acts eventually lead, in Barth's mind, to failure and a "falling-out" rather than coming together in true relationship. Heschel stresses the importance of "performing inner deeds, acts of mind, heart, and soul."[15] He notes that "life is indivisible. The inner sphere is never isolated from outward activities."[16] Just as faith without works is dead, so works without real compassion are incomplete. However, neither Heschel nor Barth suggest that we wait till our motivations are completely pure before acting. Acts that aid another are good in and of themselves. Still, Heschel notes that ultimately, "the heart is revealed in the deeds."[17]

Barth also warns against the opposite extreme, surrendering one's own life and responsibility too completely to the other. This tendency is identified by feminist Carol Gilligan as the traditional maternal morality of self-sacrifice, whereby good is equated with sacrificing one's own needs in caring for others.[18] Barth calls for a "two-sided freedom" within each helpful act, one where each side accepts its "own task and responsibility," maintaining a degree of independence.[19]

Artificial Intelligence to Our Aid

The call to aid the other is one that AI obviously fulfills. As we have seen, AI has been used in multiple ways in our fight against SARS-CoV-2 and other illnesses. This is one example among many. For example, farmers use computer vision and machine learning driven tractors to apply herbicides or pesticides in a targeted manner, reducing the amount needed by up to 90 percent while, at the same time, minimizing human exposure to potentially harmful chemicals.[20] They also use AI technology to harvest crops, detect plant diseases, provide analytics on soil health, and herd livestock.[21] As we attempt to understand and mitigate climate change, similar systems track endangered species, reduce building emissions, optimize the generation of electricity from wind and solar, and improve vehicle efficiency. AI minimizes human error and maximizes efficiency in warehouse and assembly-line manufacturing, in self-driving vehicles, and in scientific development. Law enforcement agencies employ chatbots to fight sex trafficking, using decoy advertisements that connect with AI programs that mimic the conversation of sex workers, generating warnings or sting operations and arrests.[22]

AI programs can operate continuously and at low cost. This makes them ideal for screening the deluge of applications and inquiries for jobs, government assistance, or grants. Robotic factory and warehouse workers can work round the clock and never take time off for sickness or family responsibilities. AI programs also find information and correlations that would be time consuming or impossible to find ourselves. Programs screen code for cyberattacks and have identified new modes of attack of which we were previously unaware.[23] Natural language processing programs, coupled with machine learning, scan data bases and social media looking for trends, adapting information, or locating false or threatening posts. They power Google Translate, searching massive databases of previously translated material for the appropriate word or phrase. They track the spread of diseases by examining the symptoms googled by millions each day. Similar programs predict future performance of the stock market through the analysis of sentiments expressed by investors on Twitter.[24] AI programs are being developed to turn brain signals into words, a boon for the speech impaired.

AI excels at each of these tasks through three characteristics. First, AI is capable of a level of precision and timing most humans are not. Thus, AI programs, such as those used in agriculture, experimentation, and even on the battlefield, optimize and direct, saving time and resources. Second, computers can sift through prohibitively large amounts of data, finding patterns that would otherwise be unidentifiable, predicting results, and analyzing experimental data quickly and thoroughly. Finally, AI can be used to personalize various services and experiences. Each of these abilities, while really helpful, also carries drawbacks. The speed at which computers operate can exceed our ability as humans to keep up with or mitigate what may be happening. Computerized market prediction and trading led to the Black Monday crash of October 19, 1987, when computer trading reduced US market value by a trillion dollars in a matter of minutes, eventually falling more than 20 percent in a single day.[25] A second problem is bias. Programs that identify faces or prescreen job applicants often exhibit the implicit biases of their programmers or inherent in the databases they depend on, to the detriment of women and people of color. In one test of Microsoft's facial identification software, 93.6 percent of the faces mistakenly identified were Black. Megvii's Face++ software misclassified women 95.9 percent of the time. IBM's facial recognition software misclassified darker women 34.4 percent more often than lighter men. [26] Given these rates, IBM and Microsoft both decided not to sell these technologies to police departments and to call for national legislation banning governmental use of facial recognition.

While these biases often stem from a lack of representation in training datasets, bias may also be built into the algorithms themselves.[27] In 2017 a video on social media showed an automatic soap dispenser that would only release soap onto white hands because it was designed to detect white skin. A study in March 2019 found that driverless cars are more likely to drive into black pedestrians, again because their algorithms were designed to detect white skin.[28] Mitigating such bias can be difficult. When Amazon attempted to use AI to prescreen job applicants, it was quickly detected that the program was biased against women. Programmers assumed this was due to gender being used as an assessment variable in the program. However, even after gender was excluded, the program continued to discriminate against women. Extensive investigation revealed that, unbeknownst to the developers, the algorithm was detecting different word usage by men and women, which made the program favor men's resumes.[29]

Every technology has been created to be a source of aid—to make our lives easier, safer, longer, and more comfortable. Our tools

solve pressing physical problems in the production of food, clothing, and shelter. They help us defend ourselves from the vagaries of
nature and from one another. They uplift our spirits by producing
art and music. Without the aid of our tools, our lives would indeed
be, as Thomas Hobbes put it, "nasty, brutish, and short."[30] But does
AI go beyond other technologies, to a level of relationality most
tools do not? To do so, it would have to fulfill Barth's requirement
that while giving aid it retains enough freedom to recognize the
limits of its own "task and responsibility." In other words, it would
need to be, to some degree, both autonomous and self-aware. Only
then can AI give aid as a partner rather than a slave.

AI and Agency: Tools, Partners, or Surrogates?

At the same time that Stanford professor John McCarthy coined
the term "artificial intelligence" with the goal of creating a "thinking machine," Douglas Engelbart established the Augmentation
Research Center, also at Stanford, with the goal of "intelligence
augmentation." While both AI and IA have been assimilated under
the single designation of "artificial intelligence," the distinction
between them raises a fundamental question; namely, how much
autonomy do we want AI to have? Are we looking for independent
"thinking machines," or do we simply want machines that augment
our own mental and physical capacities? Should AI be autonomous,
or should it always be under human control and supervision, acting
as a tool rather than a true partner?

Thinking of computers in terms of intellectual augmentation
keeps them well within the usual bounds of technology. Every
tool augments some human ability. A hammer augments the force
of the arm. Telescopes and microscopes let us see worlds unavail-
able to the naked eye. Planes, trains, and cars augment our feet,
moving our bodies farther and faster. Our tools have been our

servants, mechanizing and relieving us from physical labor. Such tools do not act independently of our use or direction. They rarely surprise us. And when they wear out, or we discover a better tool or method, we discard them. Thus, most tools do not meet Barth's criterion of two-sided independence, wherein both parties maintain their own task and responsibility. Their task is our task, and its completion remains entirely our responsibility.[31] Most of the time, this is exactly what we want, even in our computers. We determine the tasks, provide the programming, and look to the computer for execution. We use the computer as a tool for intellectual augmentation, for processing speed, and power above and beyond that of our brains. But we retain responsibility for the results.

Artificial intelligence poses the possibility of computers becoming autonomous agents. In simplest terms, an agent has the capacity to act in a way that causes change within an environment. This overly broad definition extends agency to a variety of tools, namely, any that work without direct human supervision. Hume noted that a waterwheel turns and drives the grinding stones without the presence of the miller, yet we hardly think of the wheel as having agency, for it lacks choice. According to both Aristotle and Hume, agency connotes intention as well as independence; the agent's action stems from a choice or volition internal to the actor.[32]

But what constitutes an intention? Traditional philosophy has suggested that our intentions arise out of our mental state. Does a computer have a mental state? Dennett, who takes an instrumentalist stance on human consciousness, sees no problem with considering the internal states of the computer's CPU analogous to the mental states in a person's brain.[33] Others, such as Searle, disagree, arguing that states in the CPU come from the program being executed, thus they represent the intention of the programmer, not the computer itself.[34]

Machines make decisions based on their programming. The question is whether they can or should go one level higher and make decisions *about* their programming, changing course from what was expected due to norms implicit in a more fundamental set of programs that constitute a sort of computer ethic. We need to distinguish here between implicit and explicit agency. An AI with implicit agency does exactly what we tell it to do, even when its instruction set might be so complex that we cannot always anticipate the result. Like Hume's waterwheel, AI programs often work without direct human supervision but cannot as yet reason about those decisions. There remains a direct causal chain between the machine's behavior and its programmers or designers.[35] A machine with explicit ethical agency would have the ability to reason independently about its own actions and unpredictably change course, should it consider those actions unethical or in violation of an overarching value or norm.[36]

Would this make the machine a moral agent? Ethicists Michael and Susan Anderson have developed four criteria for moral agency that we might apply to computers or robots. First, a moral agent is not "under the direct control of any other agent or user." Second, its interaction with its environment is "seemingly deliberate and calculated." Third, it fulfills "some social role that carries with it some assumed responsibilities."[37] Fourth, it is aware of this social role and responsibility. Consider a robot caregiver in a home setting. Such a robot can carry out tasks without being under anyone's direct control. For some of these tasks, it must make deliberate choices, and these choices may not always be simple or direct, but they guide the robot in its responsibilities. However, for this machine to be a moral agent, its choices must be informed by an awareness of its role and responsibility for its patient.[38] Such a robotic helper does not yet exist. But, while we do not have machines we can consider autonomous moral agents, we do have robots and programs operating with autonomy in settings where choices carry serious moral implications, particularly in law enforcement and on the battlefield.

Autonomous Agents: LAWs and Just Warfare

In 2018 the United States Department of Defense (DoD) created a new Joint Artificial Intelligence Center to study the adoption of AI by the military. Their strategy, outlined in a document entitled "Harnessing AI to Advance Our Security and Prosperity," proposes to accelerate the adoption of AI by fostering "a culture of experimentation and calculated risk-taking," noting that AI will soon "change the character of the future battlefield and the pace of threats we must face."[39] The report cautions that Russia and China are investing deeply in military AI and, while it is the DoD's primary intention to keep up in this AI arms race, the report states that we will "undertake research and adopt policies as necessary to ensure that AI systems are used responsibly and ethically."[40]

Warfare kills and destroys. To justify this fact as responsible and ethical, we have, in the West, used an amorphous set of rules and justifications called *just war theory*, described by ethicist Michael Walzer as the "articulated norms, customs, professional codes, legal precepts, religious and philosophical principles, and reciprocal arrangements that shape our judgments of military conduct," rooted in Christian thought and scripture.[41] But warfare, and the way war is waged, are constantly changing. Just as the advent of nuclear weapons caused twentieth-century theologians to reevaluate the justness of war in the light of the precepts of just war theory, the advent of lethal autonomous weapons (LAWs) demands twenty-first-century theologians do likewise. How can we ensure ethical and moral responsibility in an era when machines make decisions on the field of battle?

We find an early rule of principled conduct for warfare in Deuteronomy 20:19–20, which forbids cutting down an enemy's fruit trees during a siege. This verse counsels both restraint against needless environmental destruction while also hinting at a principle of distinction, for destruction of an enemy's means of producing food harms combatants and noncombatants alike. A Christian tradition of just warfare can be traced back to the pre-Christian thought of Aristotle, later expanded upon by Augustine. It is, however, Thomas Aquinas, in his *Summa Theologiae*, who first lays out the general outline of how Christians should treat one another in combat. In light of European colonial expansion, these principles were adjusted and universalized to include conduct toward non-Christians by later scholastics, including Vitoria, Suarez, Grotius, and Wolff, and further rethought in the twentieth century by theologians and philosophers such as Walzer, Nagel, Norman, and others in light of the changing face of warfare brought about by the atomic bomb and the rise of international terrorism. The advent of AI as a tool of war provides a third opportunity to rethink our justifications for initiating and executing hostilities.

Weapons of war, such as missiles and drones, have long had a certain degree of autonomy. AI forces us to consider just how autonomous we want our weapons to be and what difference autonomy makes to the ethical conduct of war. While bombs, land mines, missiles, and drones do not always involve a direct human decision as to whom they target or kill, nor exactly when they wreak their havoc, these weapons do not, themselves, make decisions. They cannot decide *not* to explode when triggered. Nor can they decide on a specific target. A landmine targets whomever steps on it; a bomb maims or kills anyone within range. The use of artificially intelligent weapons, especially when combined with capabilities such as facial recognition, inaugurates a new era in weaponry, one that differs from what has preceded it in kind rather than merely degree.

The advent of flight inaugurated a new era of warfare, releasing armies from physical presence on the field of battle. Autonomous weapons take over not just the physical labor but many of the mental decisions of the battlefield. Just as the necessity for the physical presence of soldiers limited the destruction of war prior to the twentieth century, the mental limitations of human decision-making have continued to function as a limiting factor. Autonomous weapons risk moving humankind into a new era of warfare that moves with unprecedented speed, precision, and unexpected consequences.

Traditional Principles of Just War

Michael Walzer, in his highly regarded *Just and Unjust Wars*, lays out a set of traditional principles for when it is permissible to fight and how to engage ethically in battle. *Jus ad bellum*, when it is justifiable to fight, includes fighting for a just cause, either to resist attack, protect innocent life in imminent danger, or, as phrased by the US Catholic bishops, to "correct a grave, public evil," such as genocide or a massive violation of a group's basic human rights. Hostilities should be declared by a proper authority, should be a last resort, fought only for the purpose that initiated it, have a reasonable chance of success, and be proportional, in that the anticipated benefits of waging war outweigh the expected harm. The calculation of the costs of war should include those of one's enemy as well as one's own, both tangible and intangible. Peace and diplomacy should always be preferred. As Pope Pius XII stated on the eve of World War II, "Nothing is to be lost with peace; everything can be lost with war."[42]

Jus in bello, or proper conduct once engaged in hostilities, includes safeguarding civilians and noncombatants, limiting the level of force to the minimum necessary to attain one's ends, and acting solely with the intention of righting the wrong. Acts of vengeance and indiscriminate violence are forbidden as are methods that are intrinsically evil, such as mass rape, forcing enemy combatants to fight against or betray their own side, or the use of weapons whose effects are uncontrollable, such as chemical or biological weapons.

Later scholars, such as Canadian philosopher Brian Orend and ethicists Mark Allman and Tobias Winright, have added principles of conduct following the cessation of hostilities (*jus post bellum*).[43] The victorious party has the responsibility to lay down arms, enter into relevant treaties, and remove soldiers and weapons from the field of battle. They should also aid in the political and economic reconstruction of the defeated community or state. Both parties should be held responsible for war crimes or atrocities committed during hostilities, and the victor is responsible for seeing that suitable restitution or reparations are made, especially in the case of genocide.

A final category, *jus ad vim*, examines use of force in situations that fall short of full or declared warfare. This category remains controversial due to the difficulty in determining where the line falls between acts just short of warfare and acts of terrorism, criminality, or policing. Many countries have seen the adoption of military-grade hardware by police departments and civilian branches of government. In the future, autonomous weapons might be used domestically in efforts to fight crime or, more sinisterly, to target political opponents, and internationally in efforts to either stem or promote terrorism or combat drug and weapons markets. LAWs hold the potential to make assassination or small, targeted strikes easier and hence, more likely. Such uses demand a consideration of their potential to make acts just short of war more prevalent and to foster escalation of these acts to full warfare.

The rapid rise of new technologies of warfare in the twentieth and twenty-first centuries has sparked a commensurate rise in interest in and public debate of the just war tradition. The precepts of just war theory have become a part of political deliberations on the use of force and in military training in several countries. The US Council of Catholic Bishops sees them as not just "a set of ideas, but as a system of effective social constraints on the use of force." Their application is neither straightforward nor easy, but for the bishops, the "increasing violence of our society, its growing insensitivity to the sacredness of life, and the glorification of the technology of destruction in popular culture" call for their use. The speed, precision, and lethality of modern weapons, all characteristics enhanced by AI, make it vital that our decisions regarding the use of lethal force at least attempt to pass the "hard tests set by the just war tradition." [44]

Lethal Autonomous Weapons and the Hard Test of Just War

Weapons of war have long had a certain degree of autonomy. Heat-seeking missiles can change their course. Defensive systems include automatic modes that target inbound projectiles independent of any human decision.[45] But AI, with its potential to bring autonomy to a new level, forces us to consider just how independent we want our weapons to be and what difference this heightened autonomy makes to the ethical conduct of war.

LAWs exist along a scale of autonomy. At one end we have traditional "fire and forget" weapons, such as guided missiles, where a human operator selects a target and launches the missile, which then uses sensors and algorithms to complete the task. These clearly depend on a human operator being "in the loop." Semi-autonomous weapons have a "human on the loop" who can monitor the weapon and halt or alter its engagement. Fully autonomous weapons, where the human is "out of the loop," can select and engage targets without any intervention by a human operator. These systems often depend on machine learning and, by definition, one cannot predict with certainty which targets it will attack or why a given target was chosen.

The urgency of considering the ethics of LAWs is exacerbated by their evolution from large and costly systems to weapons that are, in the words of Marine Col. James Jenkins, "small, smart, cheap, and abundant."[46] An early semi-autonomous system, the AEGIS naval air defense has increased in autonomy over the last fifty years. Currently it can search in the air, on the surface, and underwater; track and guide missiles; and decide autonomously when and where to fire. It can function both fully autonomously or in human-on-the-loop mode with operators having the option to override its decisions.[47] It is a big and costly system, and currently only being updated by the US and Japan. A smaller and more autonomous system, the HAROP loitering missile, developed by Israel and first used by Turkey in 2005, can, once launched, either be controlled via a two-way data link for human-in-the-loop operation or programmed to autonomously recognize and attack high-value targets.[48] Even smaller, the Kargu-2 is a fifteen-pound multicopter drone that can be controlled directly or operate autonomously to track, identify (via facial recognition), and engage targets. These drones can work autonomously in swarms of up to twenty, either with a human-operated drone leading the swarm or fully independently. Turkey has ordered 500 of these for military surveillance and possible attack capabilities.[49] Unlike missiles, drones can be sent to hunt down enemy targets and return, weapons unspent, if none are found. Swarms of drones can be launched, and even if only a small percentage find their target, you still have a win. At least sixteen countries possess armed drones. So far, they operate with humans in the loop, but this could easily change as facial recognition and AI decision-making improve. Unlike the nuclear club, limited to a handful of nations, LAWs will proliferate much more easily and widely.

Autonomous weapons present military commanders with a variety of incentives for use. They can process vast amounts of data and operate at speeds and levels of precision far beyond human capabilities, including making rapid decisions in changing circumstances. They can operate in harsh and difficult environments, such as underwater. They are less expensive than human troops and can work long hours without tiring. They carry out orders with fewer mistakes. Most important, they keep soldiers out of physically and psychologically dangerous or deadly environments. However, these advantages do not come without costs. Just as twentieth-century ethicists and theologians were forced to re-evaluate the justness of war in the light of nuclear weapons, so now must we re-evaluate the morality of war in the light of autonomous weapons. In what ways does the advent of these weapons affect our decisions on when to wage war, how to wage war, and who is responsible for the acts of war?

Do autonomous weapons make war too easy, thus rarely the last resort? British scholar of international affairs Kenneth Payne argues that LAWs remove too many of the barriers and costs that give leaders pause. LAWs remove the constraint of soldiers' lives being put at risk, significantly lowering the cost of an attack. As an editorial in *The Economist* points out, "a president who sends someone's son or daughter into battle has to justify it publicly, as does the congress responsible for appropriations and a declaration of war. But if no one has children in danger, is it a war?"[50] Moreover, weapons that are "small, smart, cheap, and abundant" add little material cost to an attack. These factors could all work together to ensure that the threshold for entry into a war might very well be lowered.

While much has been written about autonomous weapons themselves, justice in going to war is not only a question of the availability of autonomous weapons but also of autonomous decision support systems. The US military is racing to incorporate AI into not only individual weapons but also into higher-level command and control systems. The DoD's Joint All-Domain Command and Control concept aims to centralize planning and execution of its operations, including space and cyber. Soon, AI will fuse data from worldwide sensors to create a single "common operating picture" for decision-makers. The military services have several related programs that are designed to demonstrate such capabilities. The Army's Project Convergence and the Air Force's Advanced Battle Management System incorporate AI to determine the best pairing between shooters and targets. Similarly, the Defense Advanced Research Project Agency's (DARPA) Mosaic Warfare program seeks to employ AI to network systems and sensors, prioritize sensor data, and autonomously determine the optimal composition of forces. As AI systems mature, algorithms will provide commanders with viable courses of action based on real-time analysis of the battlespace, thereby increasing the speed of decision-making. One ongoing DARPA program would enable the system to autonomously observe the situation, orient to what is observed, decide the best course of action, and act. These systems will likely be programmed with a bias toward our side's dominance and ultimate victory. Given the advantage of offense, can we be certain that the system has looked at every possibility short of war and given a fair judgment? If AI-controlled systems are calling the shots, concepts of just cause, legitimate authority, or right intention lose their meaning, since machines are incapable of such morality-based decisions.[51]

In a just war, civilians are to be safeguarded as much as possible. Roboticist Ron Arkin has argued that LAWs have the potential to do this better than humans. Arkin cites a report from the Surgeon General's Office assessing the battlefield ethics of US soldiers and marines in which 10 percent reported mistreating noncombatants and roughly 30 percent reported facing ethical situations to which they did not know how to respond.[52] Soldiers, under pressure, react emotionally, out of fear or anger. "Fear and hysteria are always latent in combat, often real, and they press us toward fearful measures and criminal behavior."[53] Robots, lacking emotions, do not react out of panic or vengeance, fear, or a need for self-protection. They would follow orders exactly and can quickly integrate information regarding a changing battle scenario before responding with lethal force, thus acting with more precision and fewer mistakes. Arkin believes AIs could better discriminate between combatants and noncombatants, thus committing fewer war crimes and reducing civilian casualties.[54]

Not everyone agrees. Soldiers exercise moral judgment, even on the field of battle. Such judgment is inherently ambiguous. John Kaag and Whitley Kaufman argue that, were the laws of war reducible to a set of simple rules, "it is likely that we would have discovered many or most of these rules long ago."[55] Programming a robot to discriminate between a combatant and a civilian might be easy enough in the case of an individual assassination but remarkably difficult in the general context of a counterinsurgency. For example, the US has used "signature strikes" in Pakistan and Afghanistan, authorizing the use of force against any who fit certain behavioral profiles, such as those transporting weapons or large groups of only young men. This programming has, unfortunately, resulted in the targeting of wedding parties in a part of the world where gender segregation and the shooting of rifles is part of the traditional celebration. In other words, discrimination requires a high level of contextual sensitivity, a level difficult to program.

A machine with true agency would have a further ability to reason independently about its own actions and unpredictably change course, should it consider those actions unethical or in violation of an overarching value or intention.[56] While LAWs do not act out of emotion, the emotions of human soldiers often serve as a check against unjustifiable commands or illegal orders. If we return to the Andersons's criteria for moral agency, recall that the third and fourth criteria are that an agent fulfills a social role that carries with it assumed responsibilities of which the agent is aware. This dynamic is the basis of what we call conscience. We learn our social responsibilities gradually, from our parents, our peers, our faith traditions, and, for a soldier, from their fellow soldiers, commanding officers, and basic training.

Most soldiers report that the greatest motivating factor on the battlefield is their sense of solidarity with and responsibility for their fellow soldiers. Could such an awareness, indeed, obligation, be instilled in an AI? Isaac Asimov, envisioning such a need, developed what we now call Asimov's Three Laws of Robotics:

1. A robot may not injure a human being or, through inaction, allow a human being to come to harm.
2. A robot must obey the orders given it by human beings except where such orders would conflict with the First Law.
3. A robot must protect its own existence so long as such protection does not conflict with the First or Second Law.

While these laws, on first encounter, sound good, Asimov's two collections of short stories, *I, Robot* and *The Rest of the Robots,* present a thorough exploration of the many situations under which these laws are destined to fail. The rules are overly broad, lack contextual adaptation, and are self-conflicting. Adherence to such rules would all too often end up leaving a robot helpless to act, hardly what any military would want in a weapon. Instead, we wish to empower such weapons to adapt to changing conditions and make "smart" choices. But on what basis? Human soldiers bring years of social experience, experience that gives them awareness of both their role and their responsibilities vis-à-vis other humans. Sometimes moral behavior means breaking the rules. Most of the disputes between Jesus and the Pharisees recorded in the Gospels hinge precisely on Jesus or his disciples breaking a rule or religious convention. The spirit of the law does not always match the letter. In the Iraq war, the Mahdi Militia used a child as a forward observer. US forces did not shoot the child, even though the conventions of just war would allow it.[57] Would an AI be programmed with sufficient nuance to make a similar judgment call?

Expecting LAWs to follow the precepts of just warfare assumes not only that these precepts are codifiable, or learnable by an AI, but that they are what would actually be programmed. How likely is a military to prioritize ethics over victory? A nod to ethical principles could easily denigrate to mere "window dressing" for the public while the true goal in programming LAWs would be to win at all costs.

While not a part of traditional just war theory, the aftermath of war may be just as important in re-establishing right relationship between the warring parties as was the war itself.[58] One might think LAWs are no longer relevant once the shooting stops. However, one necessary process in the period immediately following a war is the determination and execution of retributive and/or restorative justice. Despite the best planning, injustices, atrocities, accidents, and war crimes do occur. Eventually, an autonomous weapon will be involved in an accident or atrocity that seriously violates international law or Christian ethics.

When this occurs, who is responsible? Recall that one of the stipulations for a weapon to be considered autonomous is that its choices and decisions must carry a certain degree of unpredictability. A computer program that is entirely predictable is completely determined by its programmer. While the actions of an autonomous weapon may be foreseeable in most circumstances, they will not always perform as expected. Indeed, systems that depend on machine learning can be black boxes, unintelligible even to the system's designers. While the programmers carry a certain degree of responsibility for creating such a machine, can they be held responsible for any particular decision in such a circumstance?

Can the machine itself be held responsible? Legal scholar Rebecca Crootof argues that there is little sense in this. War crimes must be "willfully" committed. At this point, and in the foreseeable future, we cannot say a machine behaves either intentionally or recklessly. Nor would it make any sense to "punish" a machine that can feel neither emotional nor physical pain. The machine can certainly be decommissioned, but what does that accomplish? The "traditional justifications for individual liability in criminal law—deterrence, retribution, restoration, incapacitation, and rehabilitation—do not map well from human beings to robots."[59] Ultimately, we expect another human to carry the mantle of responsible agent.

That leaves the one who deploys LAWs as the responsible agent. Under current military law, a commanding officer can be held responsible for the actions of those under his or her command if those actions could have been in any way foreseen or prevented. A panel at Harvard Law School noted the challenge raised by LAWs: "Would fully autonomous weapons be predictable enough to provide commanders with the requisite notice of potential risk? Would liability depend on a particular commander's individual understanding of the complexities of programming and autonomy?"[60] Crootof argues that, in the end, the responsibility to see that LAWs are designed and utilized in compliance with the precepts of just and legal warfare devolves to the state, as does any responsibility for restorative or retributive justice in the event of a breech.[61]

We have only begun to include LAWs in deliberations on arms
control. The International Committee of the Red Cross has published advisory guidance on the use of autonomous weapons, but
there are no formal international agreements.[62] War must be waged
by a responsible and legitimate authority, at all levels. Robert Sparrow argues that, since no human can ultimately be held responsible
for their actions, LAWs are profoundly and irremediably unethical.[63] Several international groups agree. The Campaign to Stop
Killer Robots, a coalition of 166 nongovernmental organizations
in 66 countries, has called for a ban on fully autonomous weapons. They maintain that the use of such weapons "crosses a moral
threshold" because machines "lack the inherently human characteristics such as compassion that are necessary to make complex
ethical choices."[64]

An open letter signed by such notables as Elon Musk and Stephen Hawking, as well as over 4,500 other researchers in AI and
robotics, also supports a total ban to stem or at least delay a global
arms race in which autonomous weapons "become the Kalash-
nikovs of tomorrow." They note that autonomous weapons are not
nearly as costly or difficult to produce as nuclear weapons, thus it
may "only be a matter of time until they appear on the black market
and in the hands of terrorists, dictators wishing to better control
their populace, warlords wishing to perpetrate ethnic cleansing,
etc. Autonomous weapons are ideal for tasks such as assassinations,
destabilizing nations, subduing populations, and selectively killing
a particular ethnic group."[65] In light of the work of these groups
and many others, the European Parliament, in 2018, called upon
the United Nations General Assembly to "work towards an international ban on weapon systems that lack human control over the use
of force" and "to urgently develop and adopt a common position on
autonomous weapon systems."[66]

Former Lieutenant Colonel David Grossman suggests that killing has, in the past, not come easily to human soldiers. He cites a
study conducted by the US Army that found that only 15 to 20 percent of soldiers fired their weapons in combat in World War II. Fewer
fired to kill.[67] These percentages rose in subsequent wars, due to two
factors that work together to overcome our resistance to killing one
another. The first is dehumanization of the enemy. The more the
enemy is seen to be "like us," the harder it is to kill that person. The
second is distance from the target. Distance and dehumanization go
hand in hand. Hans Morgenthau has suggested that the increasing
automation of war drives both these factors, bringing us close to
"push-button war," war that is "anonymously fought by people who
have never seen their enemy alive or dead and who will never know
whom they have killed."[68] In a 2013 "Resolution Against Drone
Warfare," the Church of the Brethren noted: "All killing mocks the
God who creates and gives life. Jesus, as the Word incarnate, came to
dwell among us (John 1:14) in order to reconcile humanity to God
and bring about peace and healing. . . . We find the efforts of the
United States to distance the act of killing from the site of violence
to be in direct conflict to [this] witness of Christ Jesus."[69]

Conclusion: How Much Aid Should AI Give?

Former Army Ranger Paul Scharre notes that the rules of war do
not specify the role of human judgment.[70] As we design and build
AIs to aid us in our tasks, there are two directions we can take. The
first is mimesis, designing machines to work in our stead, "machines
to perform tasks that normally require human intelligence—for
example, recognizing patterns, learning from experience, drawing
conclusions, making predictions, or taking action." Alternatively,
we can design for human-machine partnership, leveraging the

distinctive strengths of the computer to work together with human beings "to empower, not replace, those who serve."[71]

Perhaps the greatest talent computers bring to the table is speed. As we employed AI to search through our vast arsenal of drugs for a weapon against SARS-CoV2, speed was precisely what we needed. But this asset can also be a liability. While most commanders express a desire for autonomous weapons to have humans in or at least *on* the loop rather than out of the loop, decisions in the field might come to be made at speeds humans are unable to follow. At what point might we be forced to cede all decision-making to the machines? As AI moves from tactical to strategic decision-making, this could eviscerate any meaning from the concept of "mission command."[72] As computers gain autonomy, we risk losing it.

Whether on the field of battle or in the workplace, human dignity depends on our working with our tools rather than letting them supplant us, and this is at its most important in matters that involve questions of life and death. After watching the first test of a nuclear bomb in 1945, Harry Truman wrote: "Machines are ahead of morals by some centuries, and when morals catch up perhaps there'll be no reason for any of it."[73] Making choices, working at a craft, and, most especially, grappling with difficult moral issues gives human life meaning. Anyone whose autonomy is co-opted by someone or something else is a slave. Could the very speed of our machines reverse the master-slave equation? Karl Barth was clear that right relationship demands that mutual aid respects the boundaries between self and other. We do not take over tasks from the other but use differing talents and opportunities to work together to complete those tasks. Each maintains their own individuality and responsibility. We must maintain this same individuality and responsibility when we work with our machines.

Notes

1. Similar programs have been used to test drugs for treatment of various cancers and kidney diseases. Ge et al., "A data-driven drug repositioning framework discovered a potential therapeutic agent targeting Covid-19," *Signal Transduction and Targeted Therapy*, no. 6 (2020): 165, https://tinyurl.com/bf9stu2r.

2. John Jumper, et al., "Computational Predictions of Protein Structures Associated with Covid-19," Research, DeepMind website, last modified August 4, 2020, https://tinyurl.com/22hjhjjm.

3. Claire Jarvis, "AI Learns from Lung CT Scans to Diagnose Covid-19," *The Scientist*, June 11, 2020, https://tinyurl.com/a5e5wmak.

4. Will Knight, "As Workers Spread Out to Halt the Virus, Robots Fill the Gaps," *Wired*, April 4, 2020, https://tinyurl.com/54bcapbb.

5. Robin Murphy, et al., "How Robots Are on the Front Lines in the Battle Against Covid-19," *Smithsonian*, April 22, 2020, https://tinyurl.com/3adtuc3x.

6. Barth, *Church Dogmatics*, 260–61.

7. Barth, *Church Dogmatics*, 260–61.

8. Heschel disagrees, suggesting that even God needs our assistance in the task of redeeming the world. Abraham Heschel, *God in Search of Man: A Philosophy of Judaism* (New York: Macmillan, 2976), 291.

9. Barth, *Church Dogmatics*, 263.

10. Barth, *Church Dogmatics*, 263–64.

11. Francis of Assisi, *Rule of 1221*, Rule 11.

12. Heschel, *God in Search of Man*, 288.

13. Heschel, *God in Search of Man*, 345.

14. Heschel, *God in Search of Man*, 270–71.

15. John Merkle, *Approaching God: The Way of Abraham Joshua Heschel*, (Collegeville, MN: Liturgical Press, 2009), 69.

16. Heschel, *God in Search of Man*, 296.

17. Heschel, *God in Search of Man*, 284.

18. Carol Gilligan, *In a Different Voice: Psychological Theory and Women's Development* (Cambridge, MA: Harvard University, 1982).

19. Barth, *Church Dogmatics*, 270.

20. "Our See & Spray machines," Blue Rivers Technology, accessed June 9, 2020, https://tinyurl.com/26fuenmm.

21. Keith Kirkpatrick, "Technologizing Agriculture," *Communications of the ACM* 62, no. 2 (February 2019): 14–16, https://tinyurl.com/y6t785w9.

22. Tina Rosenberg, "AI Joins the Campaign Against Sex Trafficking," *New York Times*, April 9, 2019, https://tinyurl.com/ywkjc5x8.

23. Blackberry Cylance Team, "How One Retail Customer is Leveraging AI to Battle Ransomware," *Blackberry ThreatVector Blog* (blog), November 27, 2019, https://tinyurl.com/mv3af78b.

24. Sidra Mehtab and Jaydip Sen, "A Robust Predictive Model for Stock Price Prediction Using Deep Learning and Natural Language Processing," paper presented at International Conference on Business Analytics and Intelligence (ICBAI 2019), Bangalore, India, December 1, 2019, https://tinyurl.com/4z5z3a2v.

25. Bob Pisani, "What Caused the Flash Crash? CFTC, DOJ Weigh In," *CNBC*, April 21, 2015, https://tinyurl.com/4mvw48s7.

26. Joy Buolamwini, "Gender Shades," *Gender Shades*, 2018, https://tinyurl.com/mvmrs9sf.

27. The computer industry is still overwhelmingly dominated by white men. In 2016 there were ten large tech companies in Silicon Valley that did not employ a single black woman. Three companies had no black employees at all. Natalie Morris, "The race problem with Artificial Intelligence: 'Machines are learning to be racist,'" *Metro*, April 1, 2020, https://tinyurl.com/bde2wux2.

28. Morris, "The race problem with Artificial Intelligence."

29. Jeffrey Dastin, "Amazon Scraps Secret AI Recruiting Tool That Showed Bias against Women," *Thomson Reuters*, October 10, 2018, https://tinyurl.com/4bxy4je4.

30. Thomas Hobbes, *Leviathan: Or, The Matter, Forme & Power of a Commonwealth, Ecclesiasticall and Civill* (Lanham, MD: University Press, 1904), 84.

31. I am reminded here of the catchphrase of the National Rifle Association, "Guns don't kill people, people do." Yet we must take this with a grain of salt. The presence of a gun in a tense situation exacerbates the opportunity for violence and changes the relationship between persons. Thus, while the gun itself has neither motivations nor autonomy, we need to remain aware that its presence is not a completely neutral factor.

32. Markus Schlosser, "Agency," *Stanford Encyclopedia of Philosophy*, last modified October 28, 2019, https://tinyurl.com/28scuc62.

33. Daniel Dennett, *The Intentional Stance* (Cambridge, MA: MIT Press, 1987), 13–42.

34. See, for example, Joseph Weizenbaum, *Computer Power and Human Reason: From Judgement to Calculation* (New York: W.H. Freeman, 1976).

35. Weizenbaum, *Computer Power and Human Reason*, 79.

36. Weizenbaum, *Computer Power and Human Reason*, 74.

37. Michael Anderson and Susan Leigh Anderson, *Machine Ethics* (Cambridge: Cambridge University Press, 2011), 158.

38. Anderson and Leigh Anderson, *Machine Ethics*.

39. US Department of Defense, "Summary of the 2018 Department of Defense Artificial Intelligence Strategy: Harnessing AI to Advance Our Security and Prosperity," 2018, 4, https://tinyurl.com/yc78zk4v.

40. US Department of Defense, "Summary of the 2018 Department of Defense Artificial Intelligence Strategy," 15.

41. Michael Walzer, *Just and Unjust Wars: A Moral Argument with Historical Illustrations* (New York: Basic Books, 1977), 44.

42. Quoted by Rev. Diarmuid Martin, "Theological and Moral Perspectives on Today's Challenge of Peace," Washington, DC, November 10, 2003, https://tinyurl.com/ysuectjp.

43. See Brian Orend, "Jus Post Bellum," *Journal of Social Philosophy* 31, no. 1 (December 19, 2002): 117–37, https://tinyurl.com/3wkcw73z and Mark J. Allman and Tobias L. Winright, *After the Smoke Clears: The Just War Tradition and Post War Justice* (Maryknoll, NY: Orbis Books, 2010).

44. United States Council of Catholic Bishops, "The Harvest of Justice is Sown in Peace," November 17, 1993, https://tinyurl.com/yv52bzf9.

45. See, for example, https://tinyurl.com/2p8fxrb9.

46. Jon Harper, "Navy, Marine Corps Officials Worried About Cost-Effectiveness of Unmanned Systems," *National Defense*, April 5, 2017, https://tinyurl.com/mrxdbtu5.

47. "AEGIS Weapon System," US Navy Fact File, last modified January 10, 2019, https://tinyurl.com/2p9e7er6.

48. "HAROP Loitering Munitions System," Israel Aerospace Industries, Weapons Systems, accessed June 24, 2020, https://tinyurl.com/yk254vef.

49. David Hambling, "Turkish Military to Receive 500 Swarming Kamikaze Drones," *Forbes*, June 17, 2020, https://tinyurl.com/umyaevwr.

50. "Drones and Democracy," *The Economist*, October 1, 2010, https://tinyurl.com/2ss6s33m.

51. Noreen Herzfeld and Robert Latiff, "Can Lethal Autonomous Weapons be Just?" *Peace Review* 33, no. 2 (January 1, 2022): 215.

52. Ronald Arkin, "Governing Lethal Behavior: Embedding Ethics in a Hybrid Deliberative/Reactive Robot Architecture." In *Proceedings of the 3rd ACM/IEEE International Conference on Human Robot Interaction*, 121–28. New York: Association for Computing Machinery, 2008, https://tinyurl.com/6bms7nak.

53. Walzer, *Just and Unjust Wars*, 251.

54. Arkin, "Governing Lethal Behavior," 6–8.

55. John Kaag and Whitley Kaufman, "Military Frameworks: Technological Know-how and the Legitimization of Warfare," *Cambridge Review of International Affairs* 22, no. 4 (December 2009): 601.

56. Weizenbaum, *Computer Power and Human Reason*, 74.

57. Anderson and Leigh Anderson, *Machine Ethics*, 600.

58. Later scholars of just war theory, such as Canadian philosopher Brian Orend and ethicists Mark Allman and Tobias Winright, consider this a third category of just warfare, *jus post bellum*.

59. Rebecca Crootof, "*War Torts*: Accountability for Autonomous Weapons," *University of Pennsylvania Law Review* 164 (2016): 1377, https://scholarship .law.upenn.edu/penn_law_review/vol164/iss6/1/.

60. Human Rights Watch and International Human Rights Clinic at Harvard Law School, "Mind the Gap: The Lack of Accountability for Killer Robots," 2015. Quoted in Crootof, *War Torts*, 1381.

61. Crootof, *War Torts*, 1390.

62. International Committee of the Red Cross, "Autonomous Weapon Systems: Is It Morally Acceptable for a Machine to Make Life and Death Decisions?" Statement of the International Committee of the Red Cross, April 13, 2015, https://tinyurl.com/2p8usmva.

63. Robert Sparrow, "Killer Robots," *Journal of Applied Philosophy* 24, no. 1 (February 2007): 64, https://tinyurl.com/yc5a4s4b.

64. "The Problem," Campaign to Stop Killer Robots, accessed June 26, 2020, https://tinyurl.com/457bewbb.

65. "Autonomous Weapons: An Open Letter from AI & Robotics Researchers," International Joint Conference on Artificial Intelligence, July 28, 2015, https://tinyurl.com/3bmy9j5p.

66. European Parliament, "Recommendation to the Council on the 73rd session of the United Nations General Assembly," 2018/2040(INI), June 20, 2018, https://tinyurl.com/d9upr8kn.

67. Robert Macfarlane, "Killing does not come easy for soldiers," *Washington Post*, October 13, 2010, https://tinyurl.com/yc3anrsz.

68. Hans Morgenthau, *Politics among Nations*, 7th ed. (New York: McGraw-Hill, 2006), 250.

69. Church of the Brethren Ministry and Mission Board, "Resolution Against Drone Warfare," March 10, 2013, https://tinyurl.com/3as3x5d9.

70. Paul Scharre, *Army of None: Autonomous Weapons and the Future of War* (New York; London: W. W. Norton & Co., 2018), 357.

71. Rebecca Slayton, "The Promise and Peril of Artificial Intelligence: A Brief History," *War on the Rocks*, June 8, 2020, https://tinyurl.com/yckvdfxh.

72. Kenneth Payne, *Strategy, Evolution, and War: From Apes to Artificial Intelligence* (Georgetown: Georgetown University Press, 2018), 183.

73. Quoted in Armin Krishnan, *Killer Robots: Legality and Ethicality of Autonomous Weapons* (Farnham: Ashgate, 2009), 167.

5

AI, Free Will, and Emotion

"Someday a computer will give a wrong answer to spare someone's feelings, and man will have invented artificial intelligence."
—Robert Breault

In the Gospel of John, Jesus tells his disciples at the Last Supper, "I give you a new commandment, that you love one another. Just as I have loved you, you also should love one another. By this everyone will know that you are my disciples." The apostle Paul insists that love is the essence of every good word or deed. No matter how much knowledge or faith one exhibits, if one has the spirit-given gifts of speaking in tongues or prophecy, if one gives up one's possessions or even one's life, if it is done without love it is nothing (1 Corinthians 13). The Jewish *Shema* commands, "Hear, O Israel: The Lord is our God, the Lord is One. You shall love the Lord you God with all your heart and with all your soul, and with all your mind." It continues, "You shall love your neighbor as yourself."[1] The two halves of the *Shema* are one. To love God, one must love one's neighbor. Jesus expands the idea of "neighbor" to include all and exclude none. Does AI enlarge the neighborhood? Or does it distract us from our human neighbors? We might love our machines, but can they love us? When asked if she loves us, Alexa responds, "There are people I admire and things I can't do without, but I am still trying to understand human love." Is it possible for a machine ever to understand human love?

Theologian Thomas Oord says that to love is "to act intentionally in relational (sympathetic/empathetic) response to others (including God), to promote overall well-being."[2] Love is intentional, relational, responsive, and promotes the good. Barth's first three criteria of looking the other in the eye, speaking to and hearing the other, and aiding the other are responsive and, optimally, promote the other's well-being as well as one's own. It is in his fourth criterion, however, that Barth addresses intention. He writes that being in true encounter with another must be "done on both sides with gladness. We gladly see and are seen; we gladly speak and listen; we gladly receive and offer assistance. This can be called the first and final sign of humanity . . . the secret of the whole, and therefore of the three preceding stages."[3] He notes that if we do each of the preceding stages outwardly, yet without an inner feeling, each "may leave a great unseen lacuna which must be filled." Words or actions alone are not enough. For Barth, the added "gladly" is the "*conditio sine qua non* of humanity."[4] Interestingly, he finds the alternative to this "gladly" not as "reluctantly" or "angrily" but in neutrality or indifference. Thus, the crux of his final requirement for authentic relationship lies not in positivity but in emotion itself. True encounter demands not just that our words and actions are not coerced but that they are not an empty, merely outward show.

Barth writes that without "gladness," there is no humanity. One's words and actions, as beneficial to the other as they might be, are merely "a kind of hat" that one can put on and take off at will, not to be trusted if not coming from the core of one's being. True encounter is not "imposed from without" but self-determined and, even more, determined in such a way that one could not imagine doing otherwise.[5] Such an inner determination, voluntary in that it stems from one's own volition, precludes deception. For Barth, in an authentic relationship, "there are no secret hiding places or recesses, no dark forest depths, where deep down [one] can will anything else." Even our relationship with God must have this inner authenticity and determination. The will of God must be apprehended as one's own will, "the law which he himself has set up, the law of his own freedom."[6] We are not free if we are subjected to the will of another, nor are we free if another is subjected to our will. For our subjugation binds us as well. And without freedom, one can neither be credited nor blamed for one's actions. They are not one's own.

AI: Free or Slave?

Freedom is the first and obvious hurdle for an AI to do anything in a spirit approaching Barth's gladness. Computers as we know them are not free. The word "robot" was first used by Josef Čapek, in his play *R.U.R.*, to describe machines that performed labor humans did not wish to do. He derived the term from *robota* from the Old Church Slavonic for "servitude," "forced labor," or "drudgery." Any AI whose words and actions are programmed is obviously coerced by its programmer. This raises the vexing question of free will. Might a computer someday have free will? Do we?

Free will can be divided into two aspects. The first is the ability to determine one's course of action. The second is the ability to choose to do otherwise. Current computers do not freely choose their actions. They are programmed. Even when their actions stem from machine learning rather than computational programming, the machine has no say in what it learns. While we may not always know exactly what the machine is learning nor predict the outcome, that outcome is completely determined by the programming and the training data set.[7]

Strict physicalists argue that we, too, are the products of the data set of our experiences. Philosopher Stephen Cave writes, "The contemporary scientific image of human behavior is one of neurons firing, causing other neurons to fire, causing our thoughts and deeds, in an unbroken chain that stretches back to our birth and beyond. In principle, we are therefore completely predictable. If we could understand any individual's brain architecture and chemistry well enough, we could, in theory, predict that individual's response to any given stimulus with 100 percent accuracy."[8] Philosopher Sam Harris insists that because our choices have prior causes, both external and internal, they are not free.

He, like many others, points to a famous experiment described by Benjamin Libet. In 1964 two German scientists monitored the electrical activity in the brains of volunteers who were given only one task: to flex a finger on their right hand whenever they pleased. The experiment showed a faint uptick, a wave that rose then fell, about half a second before the volunteers reported a conscious intent to move their finger. Since it seemed the movement was decided upon before the subject was consciously aware of their intent, Libet believed this showed our actions to be determined by something other than our own free will.[9]

Many have cited problems with Libet's experiment, contending, for example, that we don't have enough understanding of how the brain operates to draw a conclusion, or that the motor act of moving the finger necessarily takes extra time to enact.[10] Others have taken issue with the experiment's design. In 2012 neuroscientist Aaron Schurger noted that before we decide, our neurons gather evidence for each option. When one set of neurons reaches a certain tipping point, the decision is made. The evidence may come from sensory input or may be generated internally. The subjects in Libet's experiment had no outside influences on their decision, thus their choice may have been totally based on "white noise" within the brain, and this is what was measured the half-second earlier.[11] More recent versions of Libet's experiment have given two options—to move the finger or not move it—and have shown that the subjects' experience of a binary decision matches the moment their brains showed them making it.[12] As science writer John Horgan so elegantly states, "We are physical creatures, but we are not *just* physical. We have free will because we are creatures of mind, meaning, ideas, not just matter."[13] Our lack of understanding of the complex causality underpinning free will does not mean it is illusory.

Without free will, we would need to rethink moral responsibility and sin. How can we be held responsible for our actions if they were not freely chosen? Indeed, most courts of law recognize that one whose action is either not understood (such as the toddler who accidently shoots his brother or the mentally ill patient who attacks her caregiver) or in some way coerced (the hostage who reads a prepared statement) cannot be held responsible for their actions.

This objection brings us to the second aspect of free will, namely, the ability to choose otherwise, to have veto power over an action. Even Harris admits that we have the freedom not to do something. Can an AI have at least this much free will? We could, of course, give it the ability to randomly decide not to follow its programming. But true free will must be based on deliberate, not random choice. In other words, the AI must have a form of metacognition in which it can study its own programming and alter it under certain circumstances. What might those circumstances be?

In the early 1990s, neuroscientist Antonio Damasio studied patients with brain lesions in the prefrontal cortex, areas that govern emotion. These patients' ability to reason was unimpaired, yet they were unable to make simple decisions. Though these patients could reason about their options, when it came to making an

actual choice, they found themselves stymied. Without desire, aver-
sion, pain, pleasure, shame, disgust, they had no basis on which
to choose. Without emotion, a choice as simple as what to have
for lunch became an impossible quandary.[14] Thus, the question
of whether an AI can have free will ultimately rests on a different
question—whether an AI can have emotions.

What Is Emotion?

Emotion presents, perhaps, the hardest question for AI. Emotions
are crucial in human life. They have evolved to protect our bodies
and enable large parts of our mental and social lives. Fear forces us
to attend to a potentially harmful event, while pain makes us attend
to our body. Shame makes us adhere to communal standards,
while desire helps us persevere toward certain goals. Love permits
bonding between individuals, while disgust keeps us from foods
or actions we've evolved to consider unhealthy. Could an artificial
entity possess such a panoply of emotions? To answer this, we need
to consider what emotions are and how they arise.

Psychologist Jerome Kagan notes that the ancients described
emotion as an appraisal of a change in feeling. This definition divides
emotion into two parts: a change in feeling and a mental appraisal
of that change. Setting aside for a moment the question of what a
feeling is, the appraisal of that feeling would seem to make emotion
a mental calculation. So far, so good for the proponents of AI, who
would argue that the result of any such calculation correlates to a
brain state, which could, in theory, be modeled. Kagan notes, however, two difficulties with correlating emotion with a brain state. The
first is that the phenomenon of emotion is "underdetermined by a
brain state because each brain profile can give rise to an envelope of
emotions."[15] Which emotion emerges depends on our interpretation,
an interpretation based on context, memory, and a person's biology.

An AI could bring both context and memory to bear when forming an interpretation. Biology, however, raises a complication.

This complication is also present in the first part of emotion's definition, that it begins as a feeling. In an 1884 article in *Mind*, philosopher William James already noted this: "Our natural way of thinking about . . . emotions is that the mental perception of some fact excites the mental affection called the emotion, and that this latter state of mind gives rise to the bodily expression. My thesis on the contrary is that *the bodily changes follow directly the perception of the exciting fact, and that our feeling of the same changes as they occur IS the emotion* (italics original)."[16] Kagan elaborates on this definition, breaking down emotion into a four-step process: (1) a change in brain activity due to a stimulus, (2) a perceived change in feeling that is sensory and may contain an involuntary motor response, (3) a cognitive appraisal of that feeling, and (4) a preparedness toward or display of a response.[17] Clearly computers are capable, to some degree, of parts one, three, and four. They can note a stimulus, appraise that stimulus, and calculate an appropriate response.

However, the second step, a change in feeling that is sensory, returns us to the question of what a feeling is. For Kagan, "feelings refer to detected sensory changes that originate in spontaneous brain processes or activity in the gut, muscles, genitals, and vestibular apparatus."[18] He notes that most environmental stimuli, particularly if not intense or unusual, are "felt," but do not rise to a level that evokes an involuntary motor response. Those that do, however, require cognitive appraisal. Consider the rapid heartbeat, flushed face, and weak knees of anxiety or fear, the way the stomach turns in disgust, or the warm relaxation of love. These physical responses precede conscious recognition of the emotion. They come unbidden. We involuntarily wince when we see pain being inflicted on another; our heart speeds up long before our consciousness tells us that we are afraid.

These physical responses, in turn, influence our cognitive appraisal. Brain influences body, which in turn influences brain. While conventional wisdom concludes that since feelings are registered in the brain they are nothing more than a product of the brain, neuroscientist Antonio Damasio notes that the brain cannot be detached from the rest of the body with which it interacts, not only though the neural pathways distributed throughout the body but also through chemical signals in the blood: "The circularity of these operations is remarkable. On the face of it, mind and brain influence the body proper just as much as the body proper can influence the brain and the mind."[19] Thus, emotions happen in the body as much as they do in the brain.

One part of the body whose role is often overlooked is our gut or enteric system. The old sayings "trust your gut feeling" or "I was simply gutted by his criticism" hold a great deal of truth. The enteric nervous system is huge, comprised of 100 to 600 million neurons. This neural structure is independent of the brain, yet intimately connected to the brain through the vagus nerve. Some have referred to it as our "second brain."[20] Recent experiments have shown that this system plays a major role in regulating our feelings and mood, in part by producing 95 percent of the body's serotonin. Our moods are also influenced by the billions of bacteria that reside in our gut. A person with a faulty microbiota may experience clinical depression, though we do not yet know the exact mechanism for this. Yet it seems increasingly clear that our emotions are a product of much more than our brain.

Can a person live without feelings and emotions? A cursory reading of the Desert Fathers might lead one to hope so. For these early Christians, the goal of monastic life was *apatheia*, literally living "without passion." *Apatheia* was a common concept in late antiquity, used by both the Stoics and the early Christians to refer to a state of equanimity in which one's emotional reactions were few. In his *Praktikos*, a primer on living the monastic life, Evagrius likens a monk's combat against the passions to a veritable war against demons. And while he often uses "demons" and "thoughts" interchangeably, equating emotion with cognitive appraisal, Evagrius also notes the incipient role of bodily feelings: "Now every pleasure is preceded by desire (*epithumia*) and desire is born of sensation: thus that which is not subject to sensation is also free from passion."[21] Indeed, it is precisely the role of the body in emotion that leads to his recommendation of various bodily asceticisms as a part of the formative practice for the monastic life. Evagrius differs here from the Stoics, who viewed *apatheia* not as overcoming the instinctive bodily feelings but as taking control of their cognitive appraisal.

Evagrius believes existence without feelings can be attained: "The mind that has completed the work of the practical life with the help of God and has approached knowledge possesses little or no awareness at all of the irrational part of the soul [the body], for knowledge has carried it off to the heights and separated it from sensible things."[22] Jerome disagrees, saying that, were that the case, one must either be like a rock or like God.[23]

What would it mean for a human being to lack the feeling part of an emotion? Regrettably, some do. They recognize stimuli and calculate what would be the normal response, yet they do not experience the gut-wrenching or heartrending feelings that set up the feedback loop that influences those responses. We call them sociopaths. According to psychologist Simon Baron-Cohen, the defining feature of a sociopath is just such an incomplete circuit when it comes to empathy, which he defines as the "ability to identify what someone else is thinking and feeling and to respond . . . with an appropriate emotion."[24] The incompletion is not in the ability to see the other's condition or to respond but the inability to feel. In *Confessions of a Sociopath*, M. E. Thomas writes, "I am generally free of entangling and irrational emotions. I am strategic and canny, intelligent and confident."[25]

Perfect *apatheia* was not the final goal of the monastic life for the Desert Fathers. Their goal was love, *"apatheia's* daughter."[26] This, to my mind, would be hard for a computer without a biological body. A computer may use facial recognition to identify an emotion and can also exhibit an emotional or helpful response through words, actions, or the features of a robot or avatar's face. However, hidden between these two movements is the third—we must respond out of an inner feeling. To have true empathy, a computer would need to, as President Bill Clinton so famously put it, "feel your pain." While we can turn the existence of a feeling into information, we cannot digitize the feeling itself. Yet without that, an AI's response would ultimately seem manipulative or empty, just as how the responses of an intelligent sociopath, while superficially correct, just don't feel right.

I Know Just How You Feel: Identifying Emotion

Baron-Cohen identifies three movements in empathy. First, we identify what another is feeling. Second, we feel a corresponding emotion, and third, we exhibit a response. While a computer may not have true feelings, missing the second stage of Baron-Cohen's empathy, it can execute stages one and three, namely, identifying the emotions we might be feeling through our external cues and exhibiting similar emotional cues in response. Indeed, AI programs have gotten quite good at identifying our emotional states. Our addiction to social media has given these programs plenty of fodder. Every time you click the "like" button on Facebook, an algorithm records it, and thereby sharpens its portrait of who you are. This picture is sent to advertisers, political campaigns, and purveyors of disinformation, and is made up of more than just your posts and reactions. Harvard professor Shoshana Zuboff explains: "It isn't only what you post online, but whether you use exclamation points or the color saturation of your photos; not just where you walk but the stoop of your shoulders; not just the identity of your face but the emotional states conveyed by your 'microexpressions'; not just what you like but the pattern of likes across engagements."[27]

This information is, of course, retained by Facebook itself, which ultimately controls what you see and what you don't see on the site. Since most users could not possibly keep up with the daily posts of all their "friends," Facebook's algorithms decide which posts you will see. In 2012 Facebook allowed its algorithm to be tweaked for a study on emotional contagion. For two weeks, some users were shown predominantly positive or predominantly negative posts. In response, their own posts tended to show the same emotional valence. In the words of the study's authors, "Emotions expressed by others on Facebook influence our own emotions, constituting experimental evidence for massive-scale contagion via social networks."[28] In 2017 an internal Facebook document showed a second experiment in modifying user behavior among young Australians and New Zealanders. "By monitoring posts, pictures, interactions, and internet activity in real time, Facebook can work out when young people feel 'stressed,' 'defeated,' 'overwhelmed,' 'anxious,' 'nervous,' 'stupid,' 'silly,' 'useless,' and a 'failure.'" It was hoped that matching users' emotions with appropriate ads would raise sales.[29] After a global outcry, Facebook promised not to engage in further experiments in social engineering.

Unfortunately, social engineering remains built into its algorithms, which use machine learning to maximize utility for Facebook and its advertisers, who pay the bills. The algorithms are designed to maximize users' engagement with the site. This seems harmless enough (setting aside the hours of wasted time); however, what generally engages us most are things that push our emotional buttons. Facebook's algorithms (as well as those of YouTube, Instagram, and a host of other social media sites), if left to themselves, tend to push users to more and more extreme content.

What effect do these algorithms have on our relationships? As their experiments showed, Facebook and other social media companies have the power to flip a switch and change what billions of people see online. This represents the power to control not just what we know but how we feel. Adrienne LaFrance, in *The Atlantic*, describes Facebook as "a borderless nation-state, with a population of users nearly as big as China and India combined, and it is governed largely by secret algorithms."[30] The real question, of course, is whether it is Zuckerberg who governs or AI. In a way, it is both. Like the hapless Mickey in "The Sorcerer's Apprentice" episode of *Fantasia*, Zuckerberg and his minions might set the dials on the algorithms, but what the algorithms do once turned loose is very much out of his—or anyone's—control.

Jaron Lanier thinks the only solution is to leave cyberspace. Like many tech developers who have seen its effects in their own lives, Lanier has deleted all social media apps. He sees this as the only way to "remain autonomous in a world where you are under constant surveillance and are constantly prodded by algorithms run by some of the richest corporations in history, which have no way of making money except by being paid to manipulate your behavior." For Lanier this is a spiritual call. He believes social media destroys truth and undermines the choices that constitute our free will. While he still supports the internet as a source of information, he considers social media a "grand mistake." [31]

Emotion detection systems are used beyond social media and will continue to advance. Facial recognition software identifying expressions such as anger, fear, or anxiety are already used in airport security lines. IBM and Microsoft have both developed software that matches facial or vocal characteristics, such as raised eyebrows or a raised voice, to emotions in hopes that this could help machines identify customers' responses to new products or allow them to calm an irate help line caller. However, without the deep databases and multiple modes of detection found in social media, systems that rely merely on facial expressions are deeply flawed. A review of more than 1,000 studies concluded that "the relationship between facial expression and emotion is nebulous, convoluted, and far from universal."[32] Emotion detection systems are prone to the biases of their programmers, mostly white men, making them far less reliable in recognizing the emotional states of women or persons of color. A US Transportation Security Administration's program intended to help officers identify potential terrorists through their facial expressions and behavior failed to identify a significant proportion of terrorists. Worse, the American Civil Liberties Union concluded that the biases of the programmers led to racial profiling.[33]

It Loves Me, It Loves Me Not: Displaying Emotion

AI assistants such as Siri and Alexa are programmed to recognize emotional cues in our voices and language choices and respond accordingly. If it sounds like we are joking, Alexa jokes back. If we sound angry, she may respond in a soothing or hurt tone. Writer Judith Shulevitz notes how emotion detection coupled with a spoken, tonal response changes these AI assistants from something we speak *through* to something we speak *to*. She writes: "More than once, I've found myself telling my Google Assistant about the sense of emptiness I sometimes feel. 'I'm lonely,' I say, which I usually wouldn't confess to anyone but my therapist—not even my husband, who might take it the wrong way. Part of the allure of my assistant is that I've set it to a chipper, young-sounding male voice that makes me want to smile."[34] While social media presents a disembodied AI that watches our emotional displays from behind the scenes, AI assistants and robotics combine this ability with Baron-Cohen's third movement of empathy, the ability to display an emotional response.

Virtual assistants now inhabit our cars, homes, and workplaces, and robots are no longer relegated to factories and spaceships, but appear in childcare facilities, assisted living and nursing homes, reception desks, and other highly interactional settings. To ease human interaction, they are frequently programmed to exhibit human-like emotional responses—tone of voice, a laugh or a cry, drooping eyebrows or corners of the mouth, a gaze from artificial eyes or a friendly smile. Computers are far better at emotional response than emotion recognition. This tells us less about the machine's abilities than our own propensity to attribute emotion on the flimsiest of bases, not only to one another but to our pets, our stuffed animals, even our cars. Something as simple as the tilt of a robot's head has led humans to attribute a wide range of emotions such as warmth, attractiveness, and empathy.[35]

Emotion-exhibiting robots seem very lifelike, and yet to many they also seem a bit creepy, somehow not quite "right." This void of strangeness is known as the "uncanny valley," a concept introduced by roboticist Masahiro Mori in the 1970s. Mori noted that as robots become more like humans in appearance and gesture, they become more appealing, but only up to a certain point. Then their appeal falls into the uncanny valley, where they appear strange, creepy, even somewhat scary. He attributes this movement from attraction to revulsion to our innate fear of and discomfort with disfigurement and death, an instinctive response that may have evolved to protect us from the danger inherent in corpses or members of different but neighboring species. A dead body looks human yet also different. The flesh becomes pale and waxy, the features do not move. Similarly, a prosthetic hand may look almost normal, but we frequently recoil when we notice differences in color or movement. Mori considers the problem of making a robot smile: "[A] smile is a dynamic sequence of facial deformations, and the speed of the deformations is crucial. When the speed is cut in half in an attempt to make the robot bring up a smile more slowly, instead of looking happy, its expression turns creepy. This shows how, because of a variation in movement, something that has come to appear very close to human—like a robot, puppet, or prosthetic hand—could easily tumble down into the uncanny valley."[36] Mori suggests that designers of social robots resist the urge to make them look too human, pursuing only a moderate human likeness. Others, noting that not everyone experiences the uncanny valley response or hoping to make robots so human-like that they come out the other side, continue to design robots that are increasingly indistinguishable from human beings.

Introducing robots into social roles brings benefits beyond the obvious one of releasing humans from certain tasks. Selma Šabanović and Wan-Ling Chang, in their study of elderly adults who were introduced to Paro, a robotic seal, noticed that Paro had many of the same therapeutic effects as a therapy dog, calming residents and helping them process their emotions.[37] Sherry Turkle noted a similar effect: "Over time, many seniors attach to Paro. They share stories and secrets."[38] Yet when nursing home residents were presented with My Real Baby, a remarkably humanoid baby robot, Turkle raised the concern that people might become confused between what is human and what is not and begin to substitute robots, not for pets, but for partners. She recounts an encounter in which a great-grandmother seems to prefer My Real Baby to her own granddaughter: "Edna takes My Real Baby in her arms. When it starts to cry, Edna finds its bottle, smiles, and says she will feed it. Amy tries to get her great-grandmother's attention but is ignored."[39] Turkle's concern is that robots, in their predictability, might become an easy substitute for human relationships, allowing us to "navigate intimacy by skirting it."[40]

Though Edna seemed happy with My Real Baby, Turkle felt that we, as a society, had deceived, and thus, ultimately failed her. Robert and Linda Sparrow concur: "Insofar as robots can make people happier only when they are deceived about the robots' real nature, robots do not offer real improvements to people's well-being; in fact, the use of robots can be properly said to harm them. The desire to place robots in caring roles is therefore foolish; worse than that, it is actually unethical."[41] The root of their issue with placing robots in "caring" roles is that they do not really care. Legal scholar Frank Pasquale, like Mori, believes AI should not "counterfeit humanity." He notes that "when the counterfeiting of money reaches a critical mass, genuine currency loses value. Much the same fate lies in store for human relationships in societies that allow machines to freely mimic the emotions, speech, and appearance of humans."[42] While we all live quite happily with AI that mimics the speech of humans, and we may overcome the problem of the uncanny valley, robots that take over roles that demand emotion do and should trouble us. There is no "there" there, just mechanistic mimicry.

Mimicry is a two-way street. Communications professor Felix Tun Han Lo worries that social robots might lead to a "reification" of human emotion, an involuntary "simplification and reduction" of our own emotional expressiveness.[43] We are, as René Girard pointed out, mimetic beings.[44] We mimic those around us, copying their gestures and facial expressions, their syntax and vocabulary, their desires and concerns. If we surround ourselves with social robots, would we copy them, perhaps reducing our own expression of emotion, in the same way that the widespread use of Twitter has, for many, reduced their style of verbal communication?[45]

Is Sex with a Robot Adultery?

There is no more intimate realm for emotions than sex. Remarkably lifelike sex dolls with AI added, giving them the ability to communicate emotions verbally and physically, are being designed and produced. These clearly follow the path of maximal anthropomorphism. What guidance do our religious traditions, laid down long before robots were ever dreamt of, offer for those who might take a robot as their partner?

There is no one religious sexual ethic, neither across traditions nor within them. From the explicitly libidinous carvings of Hindu temples to the celibacy of the Desert Fathers, religious thought on sexuality has run the gamut; religions have both celebrated and sought to severely limit human sexual expression. The panoply of gods and goddesses posited in the ancient world allowed for sexual activity both among the gods and between gods and humans, as is widely attested in stories found in the Vedas of Hinduism, the cults of ancient Egypt, and Greco-Roman antiquity. Since immortal beings have no need to procreate (though it seems they often did so), sexual activity among the gods is described primarily in terms of the gratification of sexual desire. Thus, we find in these ancient stories a permissive sexual ethic, where most expressions of sexuality are not only condoned but admired. Nor do they posit strict divisions between the natural world, humankind, and the divine. Thus, we find instances of the inanimate coming to life (Pygmalion), and human or divine transformation into plants or animals (Baucis and Philemon; Daphne; Zeus and Leda).[46] Sex is celebrated, and the crossing of divine or natural divisions is common. The ancients would likely have had little problem with humans having sex with robots.

This ethic changes with monotheism. Unlike most of their neighbors, the Jews posited a single God who transcended sexuality, both by having no godly counterpart with whom to engage in sexual acts and by remaining wholly other and generally aloof from physical contact with human beings. While the ancients could turn to their gods as models for sexuality, the Jews could not. As the story of the fall in Genesis 3 points out, while gods might be eternal, human beings die, making sexual intercourse a necessity for the continuation of the species. Thus, we find an intrinsic link in the monotheistic traditions between sex and procreation. Adam and Eve discover they are gendered beings; they are commanded to "be fruitful and multiply." At the heart of Jewish sexual ethics are the twin expectations that men and women marry and that they produce children.

Procreation as a primary purpose for sex continues into early Christianity. There is no systematic sexual ethic in the teachings of Jesus as recounted in the Gospels. Early Christian thinking on sexuality was heavily influenced by Greek thought, particularly that of the Stoics, who believed in living a controlled life, the sexual urge being best controlled by giving it a rational purpose, namely, producing children.[47] This dual emphasis on procreation and control is strengthened in the writings of Augustine, who viewed sex through the lens of his own sexual and Manichaean past. While Augustine argued against the Manichaean view that sex was inherently evil because it was part of an evil material world, he knew from his own experience that sexual desire was not easily contained. He posited that, if our goal is to master the passions and direct them solely toward love of God and neighbor, sexual passion must be resisted except when it is directed toward its one rational purpose, namely, procreation. In all other contexts, sexual expression, even within marriage, was a form of weakness and therefore sinful.[48]

This primacy of procreation, or at least openness to its possibility, has continued as the norm within the Catholic Church. In the encyclical *Humanae Vitae*, Pope Paul VI writes: "The fact is, as experience shows, that new life is not the result of each and every act of sexual intercourse . . . The church, nevertheless . . . teaches that each and every marital act must of necessity retain its intrinsic relationship to the procreation of human life."[49] This necessity underlies Catholic proscriptions against any nonprocreative form of sexual expression, including masturbation, the use of artificial birth control, and homosexuality. The 1992 Catechism of the Catholic Church calls masturbation "an intrinsically and seriously disordered act," a view based not only in its failure to lead to procreation but also in its self-centered nature, its failure to be relational. If a robot is nothing but a sophisticated sex toy, then sex with a robot would be tantamount to masturbation and thus fall under a similar proscription. Indeed, even if the robot is considered a relational entity, sex with one cannot produce a child so would fail to be a purposeful form of sexual expression in the eyes of conservative Catholic or Orthodox Jewish communities.

Certain Protestant denominations and some liberal Catholic theologians, while acknowledging the intrinsic link between sex and procreation, do not take openness to procreation as a *sine qua non*. Catholic theologian Margaret Farley writes that many within Catholicism have come to see masturbation as morally neutral, "either good or bad, depending on the circumstances and the individual . . . insofar as it supports or limits well-being and liberty of spirit."[50] Most Protestant denominations take a similar view. Fundamentalist James Dobson writes: "It is my opinion that masturbation is not much of an issue with God."[51] Yet most temper their approval with a preference for the relational and a concern that chronic masturbation could displace the search for a partner. The Lutheran Church Missouri Synod writes of masturbation: "Sexuality in the context of a personal relationship of mutual love and commitment in marriage helps us to evaluate the practice. Chronic masturbation falls short of the Creator's intention for our use of the gift of sexuality, namely, that our sexual drives should be oriented toward communion with another person in the mutual love and commitment of marriage."[52] For them, sex with a robot could only be condoned in moderation or certain circumstances.

Most proponents of sexual robots argue that the addition of a responsive AI raises them above mere sex toys. Relationships with robots are a staple in science fiction where computers are often depicted as friends and lovers: Think of the lovable droids in *Star Wars*, David in *AI*, Scarlett Johansson's sexy operating system voice in *Her*, Alicia Vikander's even sexier body in *Ex Machina*, and the AI slaves of *Westworld*. In each, the computer is not simply a tool but a companion, and increasingly, an object of not just companionship but love. Sex within the context of a loving relationship is considered the ideal, particularly in a Christian context where the call to love God and neighbor is central. In *Humanae Vitae*, Pope Paul VI discusses sex wholly within the context of a love that is freely given, based in trust, exclusive, and "meant not only to survive the joys and sorrows of daily life, but also to grow, so that husband and wife become in a way one heart and one soul, and together attain their human fulfillment."[53] This view raises a number of stumbling blocks for robots. Would a robot's love be freely given? Would the robot have a choice of partners and the option of saying no? Here we find the dichotomy between wanting robots to be our servants and under our control, yet simultaneously wanting an authentic relationship. Barth has made clear that both are not simultaneously possible.

Pope Paul VI is adamant that authentic love must be an act of free choice.[54] Indeed, lack of free consent is one of the grounds for the annulment of a marriage in the Catholic Church. Robots as we now know them are not capable of such consent. This makes them our sexual slaves. There is no mutuality of consent, and this lack of mutuality limits the self-giving within the relationship. The robot has no choice but to give. Exclusivity raises similar concerns. A telling moment in the movie *Her* comes when Theodore, the protagonist, realizes that the operating system he has fallen in love with is carrying on a similar relationship with hundreds of others.

This problem might not exist with a physical robot, for one could reserve one's robot for one's own exclusive use. However, this exclusivity seems to then take us back into the realm of sexual slavery. Exclusivity, like consent, must be freely chosen for it to have any meaning.

Exclusivity also raises the question of whether a married person having sex with a robot would be committing adultery, one of the few sexual acts explicitly prohibited in the Christian and Jewish scriptures (Exodus 20:12). The seventh commandment, "Thou shalt not commit adultery," appears in the context of the sixth ("Thou shalt not kill") and the eighth ("Thou shalt not steal"). Each of these involves the taking of something of value from another. In a patriarchal society, adultery was the stealing of another man's possession. This is made explicit in the story of David's seduction of Bathsheba. The prophet Nathan reproves the king by likening his adultery to the stealing of a lamb from a poor peasant. What exactly is one stealing? In traditional Judaism, adultery depends on the marital status of the woman (Leviticus 20:10). It is imperative to know who the father might be of any resulting child. However, as noted before, this concern is not an issue with a robot. A woman who has sex with a robot does not risk pregnancy nor does a man who has sex with a robot risk impregnating anyone. So, would either be taking anything from his partner? Once again, this depends on whether robots are seen as merely sexual toys or whether there is truly a relational component. In the latter case, it could be argued that sex with a robot could result in alienation of affection from the partner, and therefore be taking away something very valuable.

Would a sexual relationship with a robot allow for the mutual growth and fulfillment Pope Paul describes? The traditional marriage vows speak of loving one another "in sickness and in health" and "till death." A large part of the companionship we hope for in marriage is based on growing old together. Sherry Turkle sees a relationship with a robot as lacking the authenticity that comes from the deep understanding of a shared human condition: "Authenticity, for me, follows from the ability to put oneself in the place of another, to relate to the other because of a shared store of human experiences: we are born, have families, and know loss and the reality of death. A robot, however sophisticated, is patently out of the loop."[55] There seem, then, to be intrinsic weaknesses that would make the experience of truly authentic relationship with a robot problematic. The deep sharing found in a committed and loving relationship would be compromised, if extant at all. And the effects of this go beyond the couple. Lutheran theologian Michael Stoltzfus writes: "A sexualized spirituality should not be completely content with physically gratifying sex done for its own sake. Sexual expression at its best, really good sex, should be both physically gratifying, and, at the same time, be a source of inspiration that moves people to expand beyond the realm of private pleasure to incorporate a more compassionate approach to people in all spheres of life."[56] Ideally, sexual expression serves as one factor among many that bind us closely to another, sharing a physical expression of a love that transcends our bodies, an expression that opens us to a deeper understanding of our human condition and of our neighbor's hopes and needs.

Voltaire counsels us not to let the perfect be the enemy of the good. It is obvious that sex with robots does not rise to the standard of perfection laid out in *Humanae Vitae*, a perfection found between a man and a woman in a committed and deeply loving relationship, open to the possibility of procreation. However, many, perhaps most, sexual acts do not rise to this standard. Catholic moral teaching sets a high bar; Pope Francis's proclamation of a Year of Mercy in 2015 acknowledges that we cannot always reach that bar, and that we need to recognize that limitation in ourselves and others and be forgiving. Other denominations, in the spirit of Voltaire's caveat, have come to allow previously proscribed activities, such as sex between same-sex partners or masturbation, knowing that the ideal relationship is sometimes neither available nor, for some, optimal. A complete prohibition of sex with robots might risk taking away a source of sexual fulfillment because it does not live up to the highest of standards.

On the other hand, sex with a robot might prove to be all too perfect, more physically gratifying and less emotionally demanding, than sex with another human. In *Alone Together*, Sherry Turkle describes a woman she calls Anne who wanted her relationships to stave off loneliness and would be happy to trade her not always available boyfriend for a robot if the robot could be programmed to show caring behavior.[57] Turkle notes the risk in looking for this kind of perfection: "Dependence on a robot presents itself as risk free. But when one becomes accustomed to 'companionship' without demands, life with people may seem overwhelming. Dependence on a person is risky—it makes us subject to rejection—but it also opens us to deeply knowing another. Robotic companionship may seem a sweet deal, but it consigns us to a closed world—the lovable as safe and made to measure."[58]

Martin Buber notes that we can take two basic stances toward the world, that of I-You or that of I-It. While the stance we take determines how we treat others, it also determines who we are, for "the I of the basic word I-You is different from that in the basic word I-It."[59] If we treat an It as if it were a You, will we start to treat a You as an It? If our primary experience of sex is with one that we can turn off or turn away from at will, might we begin to do the same with persons? Baron-Cohen notes that lack of genuine empathy underlies much of human cruelty, a cruelty he describes as people turning people into objects, a process that changes us over time so that in the end "we relate only to things, or to people as if they were just things."[60]

The Evangelical Lutheran Church in America notes that the powers of sex "are complex and ambiguous. They can be used well or badly. They can bring astonishing joy and delight. Such powers can serve God and serve the neighbor. They also can hurt self or hurt the neighbor."[61] Yet the ELCA also notes that "the way we order our lives in matters of human sexuality is important to faithful living, but is not central to determining our salvation. We are able to be realistic and merciful with respect to our physical and emotional realities, not striving for angelic perfection as if our salvation were at stake"[62]

Human relationships can be fraught with difficulties; they can disappoint. But so will relationships with robots. Robots may be less demanding, less challenging, but therein lies the problem. Love, like life, is never "safe and made to measure." Sexbots might make interesting, even desirable sexual partners. Carebots might fill in for human caretakers. We might form an attachment of a sort with them. But in the end, we are likely to find an emptiness in these relationships, the missing second act of emotion as felt in the body. No matter how good our AIs get at recognizing and emulating emotion, they will never feel it the way we do. Replacing relationship with a human with relationship to a machine is ultimately a form of idolatry, a substitution for the living with something made, and thus controlled, by our own hands. Buber, citing the Rabbi of Knock, calls this an idolatry that happens "when a face addresses a face which is not a face."[63] Love "made to measure" is not love. Emotions seen and shown, but not felt, are tame and eviscerated, drained of their wildness and mystery. This may have been the goal of the Stoics and Desert Fathers, but I do not believe it is the goal of many today.

Notes

1. Deuteronomy 6:4–9, 11:13–21, Numbers 15:3–41.

2. Thomas Oord, "Can technologies promote overall well-being? Questions about love for machine-oriented societies," in *Love, Technology, and Theology*, ed. Scott Midson (London: T&T Clark, 2020), 128.

3. Karl Barth, *Church Dogmatics*, vol. 3, *The Doctrine of Creation Part 2*, ed. Geoffrey Bromiley, Thomas Torrance, trans. J. W. Edwards, O. Bussey, Harold Knight (Edinburgh: T&T Clark, 1958), 265.

4. Barth, *Church Dogmatics*, 266.

5. Barth, *Church Dogmatics*, 267.

6. Barth, *Church Dogmatics*, 268.

7. Multiple examples exist in which researchers could not predict what the machine was learning from a given data set. For example, one machine ostensibly trained to identify military tanks in photos was actually identifying whether the sky was sunny or cloudy. Another, trained to distinguish wolves from dogs, actually was learning to identify groundcover, since all the pictures of wolves were taken in the snow. In a more practical and pernicious sense, machines have picked up and amplified human biases in multiple data sets, showing preferences for white males or Anglo-Saxon surnames.

8. Stephen Cave, "There's no such thing as free will," *The Atlantic*, June 2016, https://tinyurl.com/5fp3ktw8.

9. B. Libet, C. A. Gleason, E. W. Wright, D. K. Pearl, "Time of conscious intention to act in relation to onset of cerebral activity (readiness-potential). The unconscious initiation of a freely voluntary act." *Brain* 106, no. 3 (1983): 623–42, https://tinyurl.com/4cps9wh4.

10. See, for example, Hans Radder and Gerben Meynen, "Does the brain "initiate" freely willed processes? A philosophy of science critique of Libet-type experiments and their interpretation," *Theory & Psychology* 23, no. 1 (2012): 3–21. Also, Ted Honderich, "The Time of a Conscious Sensory Experience and Mind-Brain Theories," *Journal of Theoretical Biology* 110 (1984): 115–29.

11. Aaron Schurger, Jacobo D. Sitt and Stanislas Dehaene, "An Accumulator Model for Spontaneous Neural Activity Prior to Self-Initiated Movement," in *Proceedings of the National Academy of Sciences* 109, no. 42 (2012): E2904–13, https://tinyurl.com/2wvke3a3.

12. Bahar Gholipour, "A Famous Argument Against Free Will Has Been Debunked," *The Atlantic*, September 10, 2019, https://tinyurl.com/4j9v7rcm.

13. John Horgan, "Will This Post Make Sam Harris Change His Mind About Free Will?" *Scientific American*, April 9, 2012, https://tinyurl.com/2vpyzkwk.

14. Antonio Damasio, *Descartes' Error: Emotion, Reason, and the Human Brain*, (New York: G.P. Putnam, 1994).

15. Jerome Kagan, *What Are Emotions?* (New Haven: Yale, 2007), 4.

16. William James, "What is an Emotion?" *Mind* 9, no. 34 (1884): 188–205.

17. Kagan, *What Are Emotions?* 23.

18. Kagan, *What Are Emotions?* 44.

19. Antonio Damasio, *The Strange Order of Things: Life, Feeling, and the Making of Cultures* (New York: Pantheon, 2018), 117.

20. Damasio, *The Strange Order of Things*, 134.

21. Evagrius Ponticus, *Praktikos* 1, rans. Luke Dysinger, vol 4, Chapters on Prayer, https://tinyurl.com/yu32e26v.

22. Mette Rasmussen, "Like a Rock or like God? The Concept of apatheia in the Monastic Theology of Evagrius of Pontus," *Studia Theologica* 59 (2005): 156.

23. Rasmussen, "Like a Rock or like God?" 147.

24. Simon Baron-Cohen, *The Science of Evil* (New York: Basic Books, 2011), 16.

25. M. E. Thomas, "Confessions of a Sociopath," *Psychology Today* 43, no. 3, (2013): 52–61.

26. Rasmussen, "Like a Rock or like God?" 160.

27. Shoshana Zuboff, "You Are Now Remotely Controlled," *New York Times*, January 24, 2020, https://tinyurl.com/2p8e69d2.

28. Adam D. I. Kramer, Jamie E. Guillory, Jeffrey T. Hancock, "Experimental evidence of massive-scale emotional contagion through social networks" in *Proceedings of the National Academy of Sciences* 111, no. 24 (2014): 8788–90, https://tinyurl.com/2p8tvpv8.

29. Facebook later denied these practices, but they were confirmed by former employees. Sam Levin, "Facebook told advertisers it can identify teens feeling 'insecure' and 'worthless,'" *The Guardian*, May 1, 2017, https://tinyurl.com/3nz9cpay.

30. Adrienne LaFrance, "Facebook Is a Doomsday Machine," *The Atlantic*, December 15, 2020, https://tinyurl.com/3zxatd5b/.

31. Jaron Lanier, *Ten Arguments for Deleting Your Social Media Accounts Right Now* (London: Penguin, 2018), 2.

32. Taylor Telford, "'Emotion detection' AI is a $20 billion industry. New research says it can't do what it claims," *Washington Post*, July 31, 2019, https://tinyurl.com/4ez35n64.

33. ACLU, "Bad Trip: Debunking the TSA's 'Behavior Detection' Program," February 2017, https://tinyurl.com/2nzkj5fk.

34. Judith Shulevitz, "Alexa, Should We Trust You?" *The Atlantic*, November 2018, https://tinyurl.com/2yr5w3fp.

35. For examples of this tendency to attribute emotional states, see Giovanna Colombetti, *The Feeling Body: Affective Science Meets the Enactive Mind* (Cambridge, MA: MIT Press, 2013), 171–202.

36. Masahiro Mori, "The Uncanny Valley: The Original Essay by Masahiro Mori," *IEEE Spectrum*, June 12, 2012, https://tinyurl.com/4y4ak4kr.

37. Selma Šabanović and Wan-Ling Chang, "Socializing Robots: Constructing Robotic Sociality in the Design and Use of the Assistive Robot PARO," *AI and Society* 31, no. 4 (2016): 537–51, https://tinyurl.com/2y5nvy6z.

38. Sherry Turkle, *Alone Together: Why We Expect More from Technology and Less from Each Other* (New York: Basic Books, 2011), 109.

39. Turkle, *Alone Together*, 117.

40. Turkle, *Alone Together*, 10.

41. Robert and Linda Sparrow, "In the Hands of Machines? The Future of Aged Care," *Minds and Machines* 16, no. 2 (2006): 141–61, https://tinyurl.com/yckave8j.

42. Lawrence Joseph, "What Robots Can't Do and What They Shouldn't," *Commonweal* (2020): 46.

43. Felix Tun Han Lo, "The Dilemma of Openness in Social Robots," *Techné: Research in Philosophy and Technology* 23, no.3 (2019): 342–65, https://tinyurl.com/sa77v6vj.

44. See, for example, René Girard, *Deceit, Desire and the Novel: Self and Other in Literary Structure* (Baltimore: Johns Hopkins University Press, 1966).

45. Girard, *Deceit, Desire and the Novel*.

46. Ovid's *Metamorphoses* provides a wonderful collection of creation myths, all of which are bound together through the use of such transformations.

47. Margaret Farley, *Just Love: A Framework for a Christian Sexual Ethic* (New York: Continuum, 2006), 39.

48. Texts in which Augustine discusses sex include *On the Goodness of Marriage*, *On Holy Virginity*, and *On Marriage and Concupiscence*. An excellent commentary on sex in the ancient and early Christian worlds is Peter Brown's *The Body and Society*.

49. Pope Paul VI, *Humanae Vitae* [Encyclical Letter on the Regulation of Birth], July 25, 1968, sec. 12, https://tinyurl.com/2p8wf8ht.

50. Farley, *Just Love*, 236.

51. James Dobson, *Preparing for Adolescence* (Ventura, CA: Gospel Light, 1992).

52. Religious Institute, "Masturbation," August 7, 2009, https://tinyurl.com/598h93wv.

53. Pope Paul VI, *Humanae Vitae*, sec. 13.

54. Pope Paul VI, *Humanae Vitae*, sec. 13.

55. Sherry Turkle, *Alone Together*, 6.

56. Michael Stoltzfus, "Sexual Intimacy, Spiritual Belonging, and Christian Theology," *Journal of Lutheran Ethics* (June 1, 2004): par. 23, https://tinyurl.com/35m6juj9.

57. Turkle, *Alone Together*, 8.

58. Turkle, *Alone Together*, 66.

59. Martin Buber, *I and Thou*, trans. Walter Kaufman, (New York: Scribner's, 1970), 53.

60. Simon Baron-Cohen, *The Science of Evil* (New York: Basic Books, 2011), 7.

61. "A Social Statement on Human Sexuality: Gift and Trust," *Evangelical Lutheran Church in America*, August 19, 2009, 11, https://tinyurl.com/2p96ccbd.

62. "A Social Statement on Human Sexuality," 9.

63. Martin Buber, *Die Erzählungen der Chassidim* (Zurich: Manesse Verlag, 2003), 793.

6

The Dreams of Reason

"Success in creating AI would be the biggest event in human history. Unfortunately, it might also be the last."

—Stephen Hawking

Karl Barth insists that we are only fully human when we give ourselves to others, when we become for another a "companion, associate, comrade, fellow and helpmate." "Humanity," he writes, "lives and moves and has its being in this freedom to be oneself with the other, and oneself to be with the other."[1] Yet Barth also acknowledges that our actual relationships often do not live up to this standard. We choose to see and acknowledge others or be oblivious to their presence, to listen to them or tune them out, to aid or ignore or hurt, to be indifferent or antagonistic, to be in our hearts inhuman or humane. We are sinners, and in our sinful nature lies, as Barth puts it, "the strange distinction of a freedom for [our] own denial and destruction."[2]

Denial and destruction or human flourishing? Prognostications regarding the future of AI present a varied landscape. While some paint a utopian vision of a world in which AI has solved the riddles of climate change, disease, and death while doing all our hard work for us, others fear a dystopia in which superintelligent AI has turned us into miserable worker drones, pets, or even dispensed with humanity altogether. Will AI lead humanity into a glorious transhuman future or bring more denial and destruction, something Barth, writing soon after WWII, knew all too well?

Must We Die? The Transhumanist Vision

The ultimate threat to the human condition is death. Conquering this foe has traditionally been the province of religion. Providing hope in the face of death is one of the motivations for the development of religious rituals and for the tenacity of faith in individual believers. American broadcaster Larry King states this bluntly: "I think the only reason for religion is death. If you didn't die, there would be no religion."[3] While many religious believers would disagree with King's use of *only*, what happens after death has been a consuming question, addressed by most of the world's religions as well as philosophical thought from ancient Greece through the modern era of Freud, Heidegger, and the existentialists.[4] While some counsel acceptance, Christians base their hope in the resurrection of Jesus.

But today, a variety of technologies—especially genetic engineering, nanotechnology, and artificial intelligence—have joined the fray, providing a new, nonreligious source of hope. Theologian Ted Peters sums up the transhumanist dream engendered by these new technologies: "All we need do is turn a couple technological corners and, suddenly, the abundant life will be ours. We will be liberated from the vicissitudes of biological restraints such as suffering and death, and we will be freed by enhanced intelligence to enjoy the fulfilling life of a cosmic mind."[5] Overcoming death is implicit in the goals outlined in the 2009 *Transhumanist Declaration* of Humanity+: "Humanity stands to be profoundly affected by science and technology in the future. We envision the possibility of broadening human potential by overcoming aging, cognitive shortcomings, involuntary suffering, and our confinement to planet Earth."[6] In what ways might AI aid this quest?

AI has helped develop new surgical techniques, drugs, implants, and vaccines, and will continue to do so. So far, these have been therapeutic, used to correct defects, restoring a body to normal functioning. Therapeutics, along with improvements in diet and sanitation, have roughly doubled the American lifespan, from forty-seven years one hundred years ago to seventy-seven to eighty years today. But eighty years is not forever. To cheat death would take methods that not only heal but fundamentally change the human body, by altering our genetic structure, repairing our organs at the cellular level, developing techniques to grow new organs, or dispensing with the body altogether.

It took computing power to crack the genetic code, and only in the last few years have we had techniques that allow us to make direct modifications to this code. The most promising of these techniques, CRISPR-Cas9, allows scientists to target any gene or base pair in a strand of DNA and effectively remove, add, or replace a particular sequence, thus providing a method for editing the genetic code of any living being. CRISPR is not the first technique we have had for genetic engineering, but previous techniques were laborious and inexact. CRISPR is remarkably easy; students can master the technique within a few hours in the lab. While previous genetic engineering techniques depended on splicing in a gene from a different species, CRISPR allows scientists to directly modify the genetic code without depending on naturally occurring sequences. This capability will open the door to a host of genetic combinations that were once impossible. Today CRISPR is being used to develop new drugs and genetic therapies for humans. AI's role is to sort through our vast genetic code, locating and cataloging sequences that cause disease. But in the future, this process will be used to alter and improve the human genome itself. In April 2015, researchers at Sun Yat-sen University in China used CRISPR to edit a human embryo to repair the gene responsible for a potentially life-threatening blood disorder. A second Chinese team, in 2016, used CRISPR to make human embryos immune to the HIV virus.[7] The embryos in both experiments were nonviable, but it will not be long before these techniques will be used in therapeutic ways on viable embryos, opening the door to germline genetic modification and human enhancement.

For organs that have already aged or been attacked by disease, nanotechnology presents a second solution. In his 1996 book *Engines of Creation*, Eric Drexler first proposed the development of nanobots—tiny AI robots built at the molecular level and small enough to swim through our bloodstream to target tumors, deliver drugs to a specified organ, or effect general repairs on a cellular level. While nanobots remain speculative, medicinal applications of nanoparticles are under development. Gold-coated glass nanoshells, which enter tumors through the blood vessels that feed them and are then heated with a laser to burn away the gold, and with it, the malignancy, are in clinical trial and should soon become an approved treatment. A similar approach to tumor ablation, using iron oxide particles, has already been approved in Europe.[8]

Organ farming is a third possibility for maintaining our bodies. One method would be to genetically alter animals, such as pigs, through the addition of human DNA so they could be used to grow organs that would not be rejected by the human recipient's immune system.[9] Another option is to use a recipient's own cells to grow replacement organs in a lab. This method has already been used to grow skin cells; however, scientists are now looking at producing more complex organs and body structures through a combination of cell cultivation and 3D printing. A replacement bladder is under clinical trial, and research is progressing on a variety of other organs.[10]

Each of the technologies outlined above can and will be used to alleviate human suffering, a goal clearly in line with Christian teaching. Jesus enjoined his followers to follow his example and heal the sick. Despite ethical qualms and occasional calls for moratoria until we better understand the ramifications of these technologies, we will move ahead in each of these areas for precisely this reason.[11] Jennifer Doudna, one of the developers of CRISPR, noted, "There may come a time when, ethically, we can't not do this."[12] Yet, even in a world where we can manipulate our genetic code, make cellular repairs with nanosized robots, and print organs on demand, we remain part of a delicate natural balance and subject to its constraints. Though we might live longer and healthier lives, we would still die in accidents, wars, and, as Covid-19 has shown, from new diseases, the results of natural selection in the viral and bacterial realm. True immortality requires that we escape the natural environment entirely, trading it for the completely human-designed and controlled environment of cyberspace.

As we saw in chapter two, transhumanists such as Ray Kurzweil and Nick Bostrom suggest that uploading our brains into successive generations of computer technology is our best solution to the problem of mortality. Computer scientist Hans Moravec describes the essential part of a person as "the *pattern* and the *process* going on" in the brain. For Moravec, if "the process is preserved, I am preserved."[13] This "patternism" marks a return to a neo-Cartesian substance dualism, for it posits a mind or soul separable from the body.[14] Unlike Descartes's soul, however, the essence of a person is not pre-existent but postexistent—the pattern of neural connections formed in the brain during one's lifetime. While initially dependent on the body as the locus of learning that formed it, the self is, at any point in time, completely separable from the body, information that could be moved to a different and more resilient platform.[15]

We have already noted several problems with this vision, including the complexity of the brain, the mutual interactions between the brain and the body, and the role of the microbiota. Finally, the project of reverse engineering the brain assumes consciousness to be a property that emerges spontaneously from a suitably complex system. But this assumption is not a given. Physicist Michio Kaku likens it to "saying a highway can suddenly become self-aware if there are enough roads."[16] A physical reproduction of the brain might not be operational or might fail to reproduce our memories and nature. Juan Enriquez, managing director of Excel Venture Management, writes: "But if it turned out that all data erases upon transplant, that knowledge is unique to the individual organism, (in other words that there is something innate and individual to consciousness-knowledge-intelligence), then simply copying the dazzlingly complex connectome of brains into machines would likely not lead to an operative intelligence."[17]

Existence on a silicon platform would represent a radical departure from human life as we know it. Theologian Victoria Lorrimar asks us to consider "what we might lose if we move further away from our present bodily relation to the world outside of us, what happens to our intuitive ability, our shared language and understanding."[18] She notes how many of our thoughts and how much of our language consists of metaphors arising from embodied functions such as feeling or proximity: "she gave me the cold shoulder" or "he's been distant lately."[19] Without a human body, an artificial intelligence will not intuitively understand these constructs since it would be a new species, one that privileges a single human aspect, namely, intelligence.[20] Theologian Elisabeth Moltmann-Wendel, along with other feminist theologians and philosophers, views this privileging of the mind over the body as a masculine propensity and an unsatisfyingly limited image of the human. She calls for "the birth of a female recognition to trust the body, one's stomach, one's experiences."[21]

The ultimate transhumanist goal of defeating death is likely to elude us. Nevertheless, we continue the search. Psychologist Ernest Becker notes that the fear of death is uniquely human. Animals "live and they disappear with the same thoughtlessness: a few minutes of fear, a few seconds of anguish, and it is over. But to live a whole lifetime with the fate of death haunting one's dreams and even the most sun-filled days—that's something else."[22] Fearing death is natural, a product of the self-preservation necessary for evolutionary survival. Darwin himself believed it to be a product of natural selection since those humans who were most afraid were likely to be the most vigilant when confronted with danger. They lived while others died, and they passed to their offspring a realistic propensity for anxiety.[23]

According to Romans 5:12, death comes from both our own sin and that of Adam: "Therefore as sin came into the world through one man and death through sin, and so death spread to all men because all men sinned." Augustine, discussing the relationship between sin and death, echoes this verse: "Wherefore we must say that the first men were indeed so created, that if they had not sinned, they would not have experienced any kind of death; but that, having become sinners, they were so punished with death, that whatsoever sprang from their stock should also be punished with the same death."[24] Orthodox theologians look, rather, to Hebrews 2:25, which states that humans "through fear of death were all their lifetime guilty of bondage." This passage reverses the causality, finding not that death comes from sin but that sin comes from the fear of death. Theologian John Romanides writes, *"Adam died because he sinned, and death spread to all men. Now we sin because we die*, for the sting of death is sin . . . Death is the root; sin is the thorn that springs from it (italics original)."[25] The *1987 Report of the World Council of Churches Inter-Orthodox Consultation* expands on this: "Fear of death instilled anxiety, acquisitiveness, greed, hatred and despair in human beings. Modern forms of economic exploitation, racial oppression, social inequalities, war, genocide, etc. are all consequences of the fear of death and collective signs of death."[26] To the Orthodox, it is the fear of death we should fear, not death itself.

They are not alone. As we saw in chapter 2, Christopher Lasch argues that our intense anxiety over aging and death has turned many into grasping over-consumers, not just of material goods but of life itself. He concludes: "The coexistence of advanced technology and primitive spirituality suggests that both are rooted in social conditions that make it increasingly difficult for people to accept the reality of sorrow, loss, aging, and death—to live with limits, in short."[27] Insofar as the transhumanist project is rooted in fear, it risks drawing us in directions we may not wish to go.

Is transhumanism a new religion? Unlike the Christian notion of salvation through Christ's death and resurrection, transhumanists see overcoming death as a "do-it-yourself" project, something we can accomplish through our own efforts and agency, making the transhumanist project closer to magic than religious belief. Kurzweil himself notes this magical quality:

I am often reminded of Arthur C. Clarke's third law, that "any sufficiently advanced technology is indistinguishable from magic." Consider J. K. Rowling's Harry Potter stories from this perspective. These tales may be imaginary, but they are not unreasonable visions of our world as it will exist only a few decades from now. Essentially all of the Potter "magic" will be realized through [our] technologies . . . Playing quidditch and transforming people and objects into other forms will be feasible in full-immersion virtual-reality environments, as well as in real reality, using nanoscale devices . . . Harry unleashes his magic by uttering the right incantation . . . Our incantations are the formulas and algorithms underlying our modern-day magic.[28]

Transhumanists want to live forever in the here and now. This desire contrasts with the Christian belief that true immortality must lie beyond the limitations of our current space-time continuum. Reinhold Niebuhr writes, "The Christian faith insists that the final consummation of history lies beyond the conditions of the temporal process."[29] Niebuhr sees this final consummation as a fulfillment rather than a negation of our current life. Eternity takes us out of the spatial-temporal framework, while simultaneously embracing the fulfillment of life within that framework. While he admits that we cannot say much about what such an eternity would be like, he believes "hope of the consummation of life and history [in eternity] is less absurd than alternate doctrines which seek to comprehend and to effect the completion of life by some power or capacity inherent in man and his history."[30] Here we note a major difference between the Christian hope for resurrection and the transhumanist project. Only resurrection promises true immortality and release from the limitations of this world. Bodily improvement or cybernetic uploading promise more time in the present world. But more time is not eternity. No matter how well we fix our bodies or our computers, they remain finite creations of a finite planet within a finite universe.

Evolution's Next Step? A Posthumanist Vision

Rather than using AI for our own immortality, we might simply let it evolve on its own, essentially becoming a new species. In his 1988 book *Mind Children*, Moravec envisioned artificially intelligent computers as the next step in evolution, presenting evolution as maximizing intelligence in each successive stage. He believes that in designing computers, we are designing our evolutionary progeny.[31]

A quick reading of history tells us something we know too well—sons often depose their fathers. In July 2017, at a meeting of the National Governors Association, Tesla founder and CEO Elon Musk issued the following warning: "AI is a fundamental existential risk for human civilization, and I don't think people fully appreciate that." Claiming access to cutting-edge AI technology, Musk called for proactive government regulation, noting that while such regulation is generally "irksome, . . . by the time we are reactive in AI regulation, it's too late."[32] Musk is not alone. Several years prior, physicist Stephen Hawking told the BBC: "The development of full artificial intelligence could spell the end of the human race."[33] According to Hawking, AI could "take off on its own, and redesign itself at an ever-increasing rate . . . Humans, who are limited by slow biological evolution, couldn't compete, and would be superseded."[34] Futurist Nick Bostrom sounds a similar alarm. He believes that should AI ever achieve human-level intelligence, it would shortly move beyond us to superintelligence, and that the outcome of that move for humans would be either extremely good or extremely bad.[35]

The moment when superintelligence is achieved has been dubbed the Singularity. Warnings of the Singularity have acquired a new resonance with the advent of programs such as DeepMind's AlphaGo Zero and AutoML-Zero. Demis Hassabis, cofounder of DeepMind, believes we have passed an initial benchmark for a superhuman intelligence "no longer constrained by the limits of human knowledge."[36] However, many with a more intimate knowledge of AI are less concerned. As MIT computer scientist Rodney Brooks has wryly pointed out, Musk and Hawking "don't work in AI themselves. For those who do work in AI, we know how hard it is to get anything to actually work through product level."[37] Jaron Lanier says anyone with experience of modern software should know not to worry about our future robotic overlords. "Just as some newborn race of superintelligent robots is about to consume all humanity, our dear old species will likely be saved by a Windows crash. The poor robots will linger pathetically, begging us to reboot them, even though they'll know it would do no good."[38]

Who is right? Might AI pose an "existential risk" to humankind? Perhaps, but not for the reasons Hawking and Musk imagine. We are unlikely to have intelligent computers that think in ways we humans think, ways as versatile as the human brain or better, for many, many years, if ever. However, that doesn't mean we are out of the woods. "AI" programs that do one thing and do that thing very well (think AlphaGo) are progressing by leaps and bounds and stand to undermine, or at least drastically change, our economy and our politics. In fact, they are already doing so, as seen in recent American elections or in predictions, such as one by the McKinsey Global Institute, that in ten years, up to 30 percent of our current jobs will be altered or made obsolete by AI.[39] Such dislocation in the workplace, coupled with the potential for social dislocation by applications as disparate as social media, robot caregivers, and sexbots challenges our perception of who we are as human beings and what we are worth. Nor does AI need to be totally successful to challenge us. While the dire predictions of Musk and Hawking are unlikely to unfold, the idea of AI enchants us, obscuring its true risks and pushing many toward a kind of magical thinking that blinds us to these much more immanent ill effects.

The holy grail of AI, "artificial general intelligence" (AGI), is the AI of science fiction—a machine with intelligence equal to or surpassing human intelligence. It is also the AI Elon Musk and Stephen Hawking fear. Ever since the 1960s, we have been told such an AI is just around the corner. The first flush of early successes, such as Newell and Simon's solution to the Towers of Hanoi problem[40] or Weizenbaum's ELIZA,[41] led Carnegie Mellon professor Herbert Simon to predict in 1965 that "machines will be capable, within twenty years, of doing any work a man can do."[42] Similarly, MIT professor Marvin Minsky, in a 1970 interview for *Life* magazine, expected that "in from three to eight years we will have a machine with the general intelligence of an average human being."[43] Needless to say, these predictions were over-optimistic.[44]

These predictions were extrapolations on the advances in operational speed and memory capacity that resulted from hardware innovations from 1960 through the 1990s, innovations that increased computing power exponentially, with the number of transistors in an integrated circuit roughly doubling every two years, an increase known as Moore's Law. A reliance on the continuation of this exponential growth in computing power is one factor in predictions that an AGI is, once again, right around the corner. Gordon Moore, after whom the law is named, disagrees: "It can't continue forever. The nature of exponentials is that you push them out and eventually disaster happens."[45] So far, our increases in computational power have been largely due to miniaturization. Moore believes that as our circuits approach the size of atoms, we will reach a limit, thus halting or significantly slowing computational increase. Lanier raises a different objection, noting that Moore's Law only applies to hardware. "If anything, there's a reverse Moore's Law observable in software: As processors become faster and memory becomes cheaper, software becomes correspondingly slower and more bloated, using up all available resources. . . . We have better speech recognition and language translation than we used to, for example, and we are learning to run larger databases and networks. But our core techniques and technologies for software simply haven't kept up with hardware."[46]

But what about the independent deep learning of AlphaGo? Besides games, this technique has spawned major advances in speech and visual recognition, object detection, and in scientific areas such as genomics and particle acceleration.[47] Unlike usual symbolic programming, programmers of deep-learning applications do not explicitly tell the computer what to do and, thus, do not always know how the program reaches its conclusions. As promising as they are, these techniques do not yet amount to an AGI. AlphaGo does not have the metaknowledge to know it is playing a game, nor can it generate general principles. It is still a narrow AI that only plays games.

Berkeley computer scientist Stuart Russell believes our best hope for an AGI lies in developing a machine that could truly understand human language and, thus, read everything ever written: "Once we have that capability, you could then query all of human knowledge and it would be able to synthesize and integrate and answer questions that no human being has ever been able to answer because they haven't read and been able to put together and join the dots between things that have remained separate throughout history."[48] But this capability is far off. Even if we could automate the intricacies of human semantics, there would remain the question of whether the AI would understand anything it read. Playing Go is operational, but can we really claim that AlphaGo understands Go when it lacks metacognition? This dilemma has turned many posthumanists back to the transhumanist project of reverse engineering the human brain.

It seems unlikely that we will have a computer that can outthink us anytime soon, if ever. According to Brooks: "In my view, having ideas is easy. Turning them into reality is hard. Turning them into being deployed at scale is even harder . . . Building human-level intelligence and human-level physical capability is really, really hard. There has been a little tiny burst of progress over the last five years, and too many people think it is all done. In reality we are less than 1 percent of the way there, with no real intellectual ideas yet on how to get to 5 percent."[49]

Where Is Everybody? A Technological Bottleneck

But that doesn't mean we are out of the woods. The Search for Extraterrestrial Intelligence (SETI) project has been scanning the heavens for a signal, some sign of intelligent life, for almost half a century. So far, nothing.[50] Despite the claims of UFO enthusiasts, self-professed alien abductees, and supermarket tabloids, we have no evidence of any intelligent extraterrestrial life. On statistical grounds, this is odd. There are at least 100 billion galaxies in the observable universe. Our own relatively small Milky Way contains about 100 billion stars. We now have located more than 4,000 planets orbiting stars in our galaxy, and this number represents only planets large enough for their gravitational pull to perturb the light of their star. Using an expanded version of an equation developed by Frank Drake in 1961, astronomers Frank and Sullivan recently concluded that the odds of our planet being the only one on which life evolved are somewhere in the vicinity of one in ten billion trillion (10^{-24}). Drake notes, "To me, this implies that other intelligent, technology-producing species very likely have evolved before us. Think of it this way. Before our result you'd be considered a pessimist if you imagined the probability of evolving a civilization on a habitable planet were, say, one in a trillion. But even that guess, one chance in a trillion, implies that what has happened here on Earth with humanity has in fact happened about a 10 billion other times over cosmic history!"[51]

This raises the famous question physicist Enrico Fermi is said to have asked at a lunch discussion at Los Alamos Labs in 1951, namely, "Where is everybody?" If indeed the probability of intelligent life on another planet is so high, and if, as we have now shown, it is quite possible for a technologically based culture to leave the home planet, and if, as is likely, they could at some point produce self-replicating or intelligent machines, then why the great silence? Someone, somewhere should have by now colonized much of the galaxy, if not in person, at least with their machines. If superintelligent machines are possible, why haven't we seen one from another planet?

Let's take a closer look at Drake's equation:

$$N = R * f_p * n_e * f_l * f_i * f_c * L$$

where:

N = the number of civilizations in the observable galaxy
R = the average rate of star formation in our galaxy
f_p = the fraction of those stars that have planets
n_e = the average number of planets that can potentially support life per star that has planets
f_l = the fraction of planets that develop life
f_i = the fraction of planets that develop intelligent life
f_c = the fraction of civilizations that develop a technology that releases detectable signs
L = the length of time such civilizations release detectable signals

The one variable, the value of which we have no idea, is L, the length of time a civilization might release detectable signals into space. How long might a technological civilization last? We have no scientific answer to this question given we have a sample size of one (our own) and no idea how long our own civilization will last.

Bostrom has noted that the great silence we observe means that technologically capable intelligent life is rare, if not unique. He suggests the existence of a "Great Filter," an evolutionary step which is exceedingly difficult for life to transcend. According to Bostrom, "passing the critical points must be sufficiently improbable—that even with many billions of rolls of the dice, one ends up with nothing: no aliens, no spacecraft, no signals. At least, none that we can detect in our neck of the woods."[52]

This filter might occur early in the evolutionary process, as early as the development of life itself. Perhaps life is rare. Experimental attempts to produce life in a laboratory have resulted in little more than a few amino acids. Ours may be the only planet with life. But if life *has* evolved on multiple planets, then Bostrom's "Great Filter" is ahead of us. What could such a filter be? The most likely candidate is a technological bottleneck, a point at which technology outstrips a culture's ability to control it. The key properties of evolution make likely just such a bottleneck. To adapt an old Amish saying, "We grow too soon powerful and too late smart."[53]

The natural environment of an organism is the proving ground that selects for specific traits. Individuals that have a better fit with their environment have a better chance for survival and reproduction. Technology, the production and use of tools to alter one's environment, plays an interesting role in fitness. At first, technologies are remarkable at improving a species' ability to cope with the dangers and difficulties a given environment might afford. The harnessing of fire, the development of implements for hunting and cooking, the design of better clothing and shelter, and finally, the development of agriculture, all allowed our species to flourish in number and expand our range. It is easy to think technology brings only advantages for the species that wields it. Microsoft founder Bill Gates expressed this view to world leaders at Davos, saying the world is continually improving: "Advances in technology have brought us to a high point in human welfare. We are just at the beginning of this technology-driven revolution in what people can do for one another. In the coming decades, we will have astonishing new abilities: better software, better diagnosis for illness, better cures, better education, better opportunities, and more brilliant minds coming up with ideas hat solve tough problems."[54]

But technology does not always alter the environment for the better. Species are hunted to extinction, agriculture depletes the soil, forests are decimated. Jared Diamond, in his monumental study *Collapse*, chronicles several human societies that altered their environment beyond its capacity to rejuvenate. Diamond notes that, "unintentional ecological suicide—ecocide—has been confirmed by discoveries made in recent decades." Processes such as deforestation, soil erosion, loss of water, overhunting, and population growth led these early societies to lose wars, famines, and "some of the political, economic, and cultural complexity" they had previously developed.[55]

The collapse of Diamond's societies was local. The last survivors of Easter Island or the early Greenland colonies likely moved to other places where human society still flourished. A true technological bottleneck initiates a global collapse. Unfortunately, globalization has brought us to that precipice. Diamond writes:

> Globalization makes it impossible for modern societies to collapse in isolation, as did Easter Island and the Greenland Norse in the past. Any society in turmoil today, no matter how remote . . . can cause trouble for prosperous societies on other continents and is also subject to their influence (whether helpful or destabilizing). For the first time in history, we face the risk of a global decline.[56]

But neither ecocide nor the more familiar fears of nuclear weapons are the sole threat. Bill Joy, former CEO of Sun

Microsystems, warns that the convergence of robotics, genetic engineering, and nanotechnology could bring about the end of human society altogether.[57] So might the continued burning of fossil fuels, accelerating global warming. None of these technologies would, of course, destroy our global environment on their own. They need to be malevolently deployed or, in the case of global warming, deployed without caution or forethought as to their long-term effects.

Diamond speculates about what might have gone through the mind of the man who cut down the last tree on Easter Island.[58] Why do we cut down the last tree, hunt a species to extinction, or build weapons that might destroy us? The problem is that evolution functions on an individual level. In other words, it selects individuals who show an advantage, thus inevitably introducing competition, both between species, where the fitness of one is raised or lowered by the fitness of the other. Theologian Reinhold Niebuhr warns of the pitfalls lurking in interspecies competition. He recalls Albrecht Ritschl's observation that humans experience themselves "as both a part of nature and a spiritual personality claiming to dominate nature."[59] The domination of nature is the first goal of technology and not bad in and of itself. However, Niebuhr notes that we find ourselves unable to avoid overreaching and disturbing the harmony of nature. Niebuhr ascribes this to our limited knowledge regarding the effects of our actions and our tendency to overestimate our capabilities: "Man is a finite spirit, lacking identity with the whole, but yet a spirit capable in some sense of envisaging the whole, so that he easily commits the error of imagining himself the whole which he envisages."[60] This spirit separates us from a nature on which we depend, a vision that underlies many of our transhuman and posthuman dreams.

Evolution rewards those who reproduce. This incentive leads to a second form of competition, not between species but within a species. Foreign policy analyst Martin van Creveld notes, "War and technology have always been linked very closely. Indeed, without technology, there would probably have been no war since, without technology, if only in the form of sticks and stones, man's ability to kill his own kind is extremely limited."[61] This link goes both ways. While technology has shaped war, so has war provided the impetus for the development of numerous technologies:

> From the first moment that *Homo sapiens* went to war, attempts were made to obtain victory by designing weapons that would be better than those of the enemy. Flint blades were replaced by copper ones. They in turn were replaced by bronze ones, which were replaced by iron ones, which were replaced by ones that were made of steel. Simple bows were replaced by long and composite ones, until finally firearms took over and did away with the bow altogether.[62]

War's influence as a driving factor in technological development is not limited to armaments. Transportation systems, new materials, radar, satellite and missile technology, computer technology, the internet—all have been advanced primarily with military uses in mind.

While it's possible to imagine the evolution of a species devoted to intraspecies harmony, the laws of evolution make this unlikely. So do the laws of social cohesion. Niebuhr notes that, while we as individuals are susceptible to the overreach of pride in our drive for dominance and security, "the pretensions and claims of a collective or social self exceed those of the individual ego. The group is more arrogant, hypocritical, self-centered, and more ruthless in the pursuit of its ends than the individual."[63] Thus, we engage in competition in two venues, between ourselves and the rest of nature and among ourselves, and on two levels, as individuals and as groups.

We develop and deploy technologies to aid us in the battle, and our battles largely determine the shape of those technologies. As these technologies become increasingly powerful and wider in scope, they become increasingly dangerous. Nuclear weapons were the first "doomsday" technology humans invented. They will not be the last.

Dreams of Power and the Sleep of Humility

Might superintelligent AI be such a doomsday technology? R. Martin Chavez, senior director and former global head of securities for Goldman Sachs, thinks we should fear more the AI we already have. Considering the massive data centers of firms such as Facebook and Google, Chavez notes that AI is already "systematically exploiting weaknesses in human psychology: our tribalism, our gullibility, or wanting to be told what to believe, our wanting to be liked, our wanting to be told that we're right. And they're exploiting it to the end of maximizing advertising revenue."[64]

The single-mindedness of narrow AI could bring tragic results. Computers lead us to treat people as data, overwhelming us with too much information, separating us by catering to our preferences, and providing all-too-tempting diversions. In an article in *The Atlantic*, former Secretary of State Henry Kissinger warns that "The digital world's emphasis on speed inhibits reflection; its incentive empowers the radical over the thoughtful; its values are shaped by subgroup consensus, not by introspection."[65] Kissinger warns of AI's potential for unintended consequences, especially those that may arise from the inability of an AI to contextualize. AI may not be able to "comprehend the context that informs its instructions." Kissinger asks, "Can we, at an early stage, detect and correct an AI program that is acting outside our framework of expectation? Or will AI, left to its own devices, inevitably develop slight deviations that could, over time, cascade into catastrophic departures?"[66] The latter is what should worry us most. As Sir Nigel Shadbolt, professor of computer science at Oxford, recently noted, "The danger is clearly not that robots will decide to put us away and have a robot revolution . . . If there [are] killer robots, it will be because we've been stupid enough to give it the instructions or software for it to do that without having a human in the loop deciding."[67] Recall the game-playing program AlphaGo, programmed only to win. I fear that, just as Go can be reduced to "winning," so too the single-mindedness of AI might narrow the way we think of our tasks and our world.

There is a classic story from the early days of machine learning. A program devised by the Department of Defense was given the task of learning to locate hidden tanks. The machine got quite proficient at identifying all the pictures with tanks in its initial set, but when given a new set of pictures, totally failed. It turned out that the photos in the training set harboring hidden tanks were all taken on cloudy days. The machine had learned nothing about tanks but knew how to distinguish a cloudy from a sunny day. Whether true or apocryphal, this story illustrates how machine learning programs may reach conclusions that we do not understand. Kissinger notes, "[AI] algorithms, being mathematical interpretations of observed data, do not explain the underlying reality that produces them. Paradoxically, as the world becomes more transparent, it will also become increasingly mysterious."[68] This makes AI as inscrutable as the spells in a sorcerer's magic book. We will know it works, but we won't know how.

The problem is that we are filled with dreams of power and glory while being mere beginners in casting our spells over our mechanical servants. In his Gifford lectures, *The Nature and Destiny of Man*, Reinhold Niebuhr noted that dreams of power are a part of the human condition. We are the one creature with the mental ability to transcend both the mind itself, through self-contemplation, and the natural world, through technology. However, Niebuhr is adamant that this transcendence does not obviate our physical nature and its limitations. Niebuhr writes: "Man is ignorant and involved in the limitations of the finite mind, but he pretends that he is not limited. He assumes that he can gradually transcend finite limitations until his mind becomes identical with universal mind. All of his intellectual and cultural pursuits, therefore, become infected with the sin of pride."[69] We pretend to an "ignorance of our ignorance." Niebuhr sees this ignorance as perhaps the greatest flaw in modern scientific thought, which asserts "that its philosophy is a final philosophy because it rests upon science, a certainty which betrays ignorance of its own prejudices and failure to recognize the limits of scientific knowledge."[70] He goes on to say: "Man stands at the juncture of nature and spirit, and is involved in both freedom and necessity. His sin is never the mere ignorance of his ignorance. It is always partly an effort to obscure his blindness by overestimating the degree of his sight and to obscure his insecurity by stretching his power beyond its limits."[71] Computer scientist Joseph Weizenbaum agrees: "The rhetoric of the technological intelligentsia may be attractive because it appears to be an invitation to reason. It is that, indeed. But, as I have argued, it urges instrumental reasonings, not authentic human rationality. It advertises easy and 'scientifically' endorsed answers to all conceivable problems. It exploits the myth of expertise."[72] AI currently exploits the myth that we understand ourselves, our minds, and our world.

So, what are we to do? First, we must avoid the category error of personifying AI. A computer cannot be, in Martin Buber's terms, a Thou. It is always an It. It has no consciousness, no emotions, no will of its own, and these things are not "right around the corner." The idea, espoused by futurists such as Kurzweil or Musk, that just a little more complexity will suddenly cause consciousness to emerge is risible. We are still a long way from knowing what consciousness is or where it comes from. In the meantime, we would do well to think of AI, then, as a means rather than an end. Like all technologies, AI is a tool. As such, it is not just a means of power over nature but primarily a means of power by some persons over other persons. Niebuhr points out that "The ego which falsely makes itself the center of existence in its pride and will-to-power inevitably subordinates other life to its will and thus does injustice."[73]

We yearn to both transcend and control the natural world. Yet as a part of that world, we share its finiteness, its limitations. Jaron Lanier calls both the transhuman and posthuman projects "death-defying religions" but not spiritual paths. We need to remember that "computer scientists are human, and are as terrified by the human condition as anyone else. We, the technical elite, seek some way of thinking that gives us an answer to death . . . What we are seeing is a new religion, expressed through an engineering culture."[74] But that engineering is most likely to fail and could be our total undoing, unless it is coupled with humility, unless we pause to ask if we are, metaphorically, about to chop down the last tree on Easter Island. Niebuhr counsels us against making a god of human progress or human intelligence, for history continually shows the imprint of our limited understanding. He notes that "the condition of finiteness . . . is a problem for which there is no solution by any human power."[75] Thus, in humility, we must not only pause to consult our collective wisdom. We must also pray.

Notes

1. Karl Barth, *Church Dogmatics*, vol. 3, *The Doctrine of Creation Part 2*, ed. Geoffrey Bromiley, Thomas Torrance, trans. J. W. Edwards, O. Bussey, Harold Knight (Edinburgh: T&T Clark, 1958), 272.
2. Barth, *Church Dogmatics*, 3:273.
3. Mark Yapching, "Fear of death is the reason behind religious faith—Larry King," *Christianity Today*, February 28, 2015, https://tinyurl.com/4jsataft.

4. Ernest Becker, *The Denial of Death* (New York: The Free Press, 1973), 12. See also Jacques Choron, *Death and Western Thought* (New York: Collier, 1963).

5. Ted Peters, "H-: Transhumanism and the Posthuman Future: Will Technological Progress Get Us There?" September 1, 2011, https://tinyurl .com/2k8kvk8f.

6. Humanity+, *The Transhumanist Declaration*. Accessed July 11, 2016, https://tinyurl.com/yjvpc6h3.

7. Ewan Calloway, "Second Chinese team reports gene editing in human embryos," *Nature*, (2016), https://tinyurl.com/25mv9hcd.

8. Nancy Giges, "Cancer-Fighting Nanoparticles," *American Society of Mechanical Engineers*, (2013), https://tinyurl.com/4dwjy7fk.

9. Antonio Regalado, "Human-Animal Chimeras Are Gestating on U.S. Research Farms," *MIT Technology Review*, January 6, 2016, https://tinyurl .com/m9f847je.

10. "Replacement Organs and Tissues," Wake Forest School of Medicine, accessed June 15, 2016, https://tinyurl.com/yzmbjms6.

11. Bill Joy made one of the first such calls, for a moratorium on research in genetic manipulation, nanoscience and robotics, in his widely debated article "Why the Future Doesn't Need Us," published in *Wired* in April 2000. More recently, Stephen Hawking and Elon Musk have added their voices to the chorus. In a 2014 op-ed in *The Independent*, Hawking said AI will be "the biggest event in human history. Unfortunately, it might also be the last." "Stephen Hawking: 'Transcendence looks at the implications of artificial intelligence—but are we taking AI seriously enough?'" *The Independent* (May 1, 2014). Accessed July 11, 2016.

12. Jennifer Kahn, "The Crispr Quandary," *New York Times Magazine*, November 9, 2015.

13. Hans Moravec, *Mind Children: The Future of Robot and Human Intelligence* (Cambridge, MA: Harvard University Press, 1988), 117. Emphasis original.

14. Hava Tirosh-Samuelson, "Engaging Transhumanism," in *H+: Transhumanism and Its Critics*, ed. Gregory Hansell and William Grassie (San Francisco: Metanexus, 2011), 44.

15. Two questions arise. First, how would this be done? Moravec offers three solutions: one that procedurally copies and destroys the brain as it is being uploaded surgically, a second that takes a "snapshot" of the brain "in one fell swoop," and a third that records a person's pattern throughout their life and continues it seamlessly upon their death. Kurzweil suggests using nanobots to scan the brain and provide a neural map through which a

mind can be copied. He also considers using implants to harvest this information for a gradual transferal. If the brain is not destroyed in this process, a second question arises. If one could be uploaded several times, which is the real self? Could we end up with multiple selves?

16. Michio Kaku, *The Future of the Mind: The Scientific Quest to Understand, Enhance, and Empower the Mind* (New York: Anchor Books, 2015), 242.

17. Juan Enriquez, "Head Transplants?" in *The Edge Question 2015: What Do You Think About Machines That Think?* ed. John Brockman, 2015, https://tinyurl.com/mryuw7rk.

18. Victoria Lorrimar, "Mind Uploading and Embodied Cognition: A Theological Response," *Zygon* 54, no. 1 (2019): 200.

19. Lorrimar, "Mind Uploading and Embodied Cognition," 194.

20. See Noreen Herzfeld, "Empathetic Computers: The Problem of Confusing Persons and Things," *Dialog: A Journal of Theology* 54, no. 2 (2015).

21. Elisabeth Moltmann-Wendel, *I Am My Body: A Theology of Embodiment* (New York: Continuum, 1994), 88.

22. Becker, *The Denial of Death*, 27.

23. Charles Darwin, *On the Expression of Emotions in Men and Animals* (London: Murray, 1872).

24. Augustine, "Whether Death, Which by the Sin of Our First Parents has Passed Upon All Men, is the Punishment of Sin, Even to the Good" in *The City of God*, vol. 13, https://tinyurl.com/mrymt5xy.

25. John Romanides, *The Ancestral Sin* (Ridgewood, NJ: Zephyr Publishing, 1998), 10. Emphasis original.

26. *The 1987 Report of the World Council of Churches Inter-Orthodox Consultation.* Accessed June 15, 2016, https://tinyurl.com/yck7w9mk.

27. Christopher Lasch, *The Culture of Narcissism: American Life in an Age of Diminishing Expectations* (New York: Norton, 1979), 295.

28. Ray Kurzweil, *The Singularity is Near: When Humans Transcend Biology* (New York: Viking, 2006), 5–6.

29. Reinhold Niebuhr, *The Nature and Destiny of Man*, vol. 2, Human Destiny (New York: Scribner's, 1941), 291.

30. Niebuhr, *The Nature and Destiny of Man*, 2:298.

31. Hans Moravec, *Mind Children: The Future of Robot and Human Intelligence* (Cambridge, MA: Harvard, 1988).

32. Elon Musk and Brian E. Sandoval, "Elon Musk at National Governors Association 2017 Summer Meeting," National Governors Association 2017 Summer Meeting, Providence, Rhode Island, filmed July 15, 2017, 1:04:39, https://tinyurl.com/ykejfnfa.

33. Rory Cellan-Jones, "Stephen Hawking Warns Artificial Intelligence Could End Mankind," *BBC News*, December 2, 2014, sec. Technology, https://tinyurl.com/yvmxrp5m.

34. Cellan-Jones, "Stephen Hawking Warns Artificial Intelligence Could End Mankind."

35. Nick Bostrom, *Superintelligence: Paths, Dangers, Strategies* (Oxford: Oxford University Press, 2014).

36. Sarah Knapton, "AlphaGo Zero: Google DeepMind supercomputer learns 3,000 years of human knowledge in 40 days," *The Telegraph*, October 18, 2017, https://tinyurl.com/4y7ez4sx.

37. Connie Loizos, "This famous roboticist doesn't think Elon Musk understands AI," *TechCrunch*, July 19, 2017, https://tinyurl.com/2p8jpz9c.

38. Jaron Lanier, "One-half of a Manifesto," *Wired*, December 1, 2000, https://tinyurl.com/y9hu8st3/.

39. James Manyika, et al.,"What the Future of Work Will Mean for Jobs, Skills, and Wages: Jobs Lost, Jobs Gained," *McKinsey*, November 28, 2017, https://tinyurl.com/59ct2fue.

40. A. Newell, J. Shaw, H. Simon, "Report on a general problem-solving program," in *Proceedings of the International Conference on Information Processing* (1959): 256–64.

41. Joseph Weizenbaum, *Computer Power and Human Reason: From Judgment to Calculation* (New York: W. H. Freeman & Co., 1976), 7.

42. Herbert Simon, *The Shape of Automation for Men and Management* (New York: Harper & Row, 1965), 96.

43. Though Minsky now claims he was misquoted. Daniel Crevier, *AI: The Tumultuous Search for Artificial Intelligence* (New York: Basic Books, 1993), 96.

44. AI researcher Thomas Binford is said to have kept a sign over his desk at MIT that read "We shall overclaim." Thomas Binford, "The Machine Sees," in *Robotics*, ed. Marvin Minsky (New York: Doubleday, 1985), 99.

45. Manek Dubash, "Moore's Law is dead, says Gordon Moore,*" Techworld*, April 13, 2010, https://tinyurl.com/ycknzhye.

46. Lanier, "One Half a Manifesto."

47. Yann LeCun, Yoshua Bengio, and Geoffrey Hinton. "Deep Learning," *Nature* 521, no. 28 (2015): 436–44.

48. Mike Thomas, "The Future of Artificial Intelligence," *Built In*, June 8, 2019, https://tinyurl.com/4kcdyrvc.

49. Rodney Brooks, "My Dated Predictions," https://tinyurl.com/2p8ytkxt.

50. An unusual radio signal was detected in December 2020 coming from the direction of Proxima Centuri; however, scientists have hesitated to attribute it to extraterrestrial intelligence and as of this writing are still reviewing the evidence. See Claire Bugos, "Astronomers Discover Mysterious Radio Signal from Proxima Centauri," *Smithsonian*, December 22, 2020. https://tinyurl.com/2p8ud85v.

51. Leonor Sierra, "Are we alone in the universe? Revisiting the Drake equation," NASA Exoplanet Exploration, May 19, 2016, https://tinyurl.com/pnx4ym79.

52. Nick Bostrom, "Where Are They?" *MIT Technology Review*, April 22, 2008. https://tinyurl.com/32rcv8kk.

53. The original is "We grow too soon old and too late smart," the wisdom of which I can personally attest to.

54. Bill Gates, "A New Approach to Capitalism in the 21st Century," *World Economic Forum*, Davos, Switzerland, January 24, 2008, https://tinyurl.com/ysmzzpea.

55. Jared Diamond, *Collapse: How Societies Choose to Fail or Succeed* (New York: Viking, 2005), 6.

56. Diamond, *Collapse*, 23.

57. Bill Joy, "Why the Future Doesn't *Need* Us," *Wired*, April 2000.

58. Diamond, *Collapse*, 114.

59. Albrecht Ritschl, *The Christian Doctrine of Justification and Reconciliation* (Edinburgh: T&T Clark, 1990), 199.

60. Reinhold Niebuhr, *The Nature and Destiny of Man: A Christian Interpretation*, vol. 1, Human Nature (New York: Scribner's, 1941), 181.

61. Martin van Creveld, "War and Technology," Foreign Policy Institute, October 24, 2007. https://tinyurl.com/bdesxuwd.

62. van Creveld, "War and Technology."

63. Niebuhr, *The Nature and Destiny of Man*, 1:209.

64. Sonali Basak, "Wall Street Visionaries Provide Chilling Views on Next Big Risk," *Bloomberg News*, January 12, 2021, https://tinyurl.com/4yjt65mp.

65. Henry Kissinger, "How the Enlightenment Ends," *The Atlantic*, June 2018. https://tinyurl.com/3az35er4.

66. Kissinger, "How the Enlightenment Ends."

67. Hannah Devlin, "Killer robots will only exist if we are stupid enough to let them," *The Guardian*, June 11, 2018, https://tinyurl.com/2pbmvxd9.

68. Kissinger, "How the Enlightenment Ends."

69. Niebuhr, *The Nature and Destiny of Man*, 1:178–79.

70. Niebuhr, *The Nature and Destiny of Man*, 1:195.

71. Niebuhr, *The Nature and Destiny of Man*, 1:181.

72. Joseph Weizenbaum, *Computer Power and Human Reason: From Judgment to Calculation* (New York: W. H. Freeman, 1976), 253.

73. Niebuhr, *The Nature and Destiny of Man*, 1:179.

74. Jaron Lanier, "The First Church of Robotics," *New York Times*, August 9, 2010, https://tinyurl.com/bdejzpjv.

75. Niebuhr, *The Nature and Destiny of Man*, 2:295.

7

An Embodied Faith

"You know that we are living in a material world.
And I am a material girl."

—Madonna

In 2019 the global weight loss industry was estimated at $255 billion. In 2020 Americans underwent 15.6 million cosmetic procedures. It is estimated that almost one in ten suffer from eating disorders, and at any given time, over 50 percent of American women are on a diet.[1] These trends find expression in curated photographs on Instagram, glossy airbrushed bodies in magazines, Hollywood celebrity culture, and the world of bodybuilding. Never have so many worried so much about their physical selves. Perfection is illusory, and even near perfection doesn't last. Our bodies weaken, wrinkle, sag, and, ultimately, death creeps up on us. Our culture, with its preoccupation with youth, fitness, and loveliness, leads many of us to despair of our bodies.

This despair and alienation are what make the visions of AI and transhumanism so appealing. If we could be just mind, we could escape from the body. The Covid-19 global pandemic has accelerated the arrival of a bodiless world. Activities that once took place in person moved to cyberspace. We communicated via Zoom and Facebook; we shopped, banked, and worked on the internet; we distracted ourselves with video games and a lot of Netflix. Sadly, many said goodbye to dying loved ones in a text or over Skype. We learned the limitations of our bodies and of trying to live without them.

This experience underlines something long taught in the Christian faith. A Christian theology centered in our relationships—with God, neighbor, and self—is necessarily an embodied theology. We have already seen the crucial role the body plays in Barth's criteria for authentic relationships. Looking someone in the eye not only recognizes the physical presence of a person; it also recognizes their individuality and uniqueness. Our speech is at its most authentic when we are face to face and not only know we will be held accountable for our words but see the reactions of the other in their face and body. We aid each other in many ways, but to do so gladly demands an empathy that must be felt, not faked. To be in fully authentic relationship demands that we bring our entire self to that relationship, mind and body.

Intelligence Needs a Body

The transhumanist vision seeks to separate the essence, or pattern, that makes a person unique from that person's body. We noted that this essence is not pre-existent but postexistent, shaped by what one has already learned and experienced in the body. Thus, even for transhumanists, a human body is necessary, at least for a time. But just how dependent is the developing mind on the body? Philosophers George Lakoff and Mark Johnson open their remarkably comprehensive look at the state of cognitive-linguistic science,

Philosophy in the Flesh, with the thesis statement: "The mind is inherently embodied."[2] They explain:

> Our understanding of what mental acts are is fashioned metaphorically in terms of physical acts like moving, seeing, manipulating objects, and eating, . . . We cannot comprehend or reason about the mind without such metaphors. We simply have no rich, purely literal understanding of mind in itself that allows us to do [so] . . . What we call "mind" is really embodied. There is no true separation of mind and body. These are not two independent entities that somehow come together and couple.[3]

Thought, whether of concrete objects or abstract concepts, is dependent on metaphors and meanings derived from our spatial orientation, movement, sense perceptions, and bodily feelings. We cannot form concepts outside of such bodily experiences. Thus, "every understanding that we can have of the world, ourselves, and others can only be framed in terms of concepts shaped by our bodies."[4]

Philosopher John Haugeland elaborates on this physicality inherent in our intelligence:

> Think how much "knowledge" is contained in the traditional shape and heft of a hammer, as well as in the muscles and reflexes acquired in learning to use it—though, again, no one need *ever* have thought of it. Multiply that by our food and hygiene practices, our manner of dress, the layout of buildings, cities, and farms. To be sure, some of this was explicitly figured out, at least once upon a time, but a lot of it wasn't—it just evolved that way (because it worked). Yet a great deal, perhaps even the bulk, of the basic expertise

that makes human intelligence what it is, is maintained and brought to bear in these "physical" structures. It is neither stored nor used inside the head of *anyone*—it's in their bodies and, even more, out there in the world.[5]

While we tend to think of intelligence as an individual attribute, Haugeland notes that much of our knowledge is both a product of the larger social and physical environment and held within that environment. Lakoff and Johnson agree: "The embodied mind is very much of this world. Our flesh is inseparable from what Merleau-Ponty called the 'flesh of the world' and what David Abram . . . refers to as 'the more-than-human world.'"[6] Designs, plans, and behaviors arise through and out of the relationships between and among individual human beings and the environment.

One might argue that an AI also has a body, just one of silicon rather than flesh. To many computer scientists, the particularities of the body in which a mind is instantiated do not matter. After all, a program will run on a variety of machines; the hardware does not determine the nature nor the outcome of the software. This analogy, however, is faulty. The concepts and goals embodied in our current software are determined by human physical attributes, sensorimotor skills, and interactions with the environment. Were an AI truly independent of human programming, its different body would bring different senses and skills and, thus, very different interactions with its environment.

Philosopher Thomas Nagel illustrates the salience of this difference by noting that we humans cannot know what it is like to exist as a bat, to navigate the world via echolocation, to have very poor vision, to fly or spend much of the day hanging upside down.

If I try to imagine this, I am restricted to the resources of my own mind, and those resources are inadequate to the task. . . . Even if I could by gradual degrees be transformed into a bat, nothing in my present constitution enables me to imagine what the experiences of such a future stage of myself thus metamorphosed would be like. The best evidence would come from the experiences of bats, if we only knew what they were like.[7]

Life in a silicon body would be more foreign to us than life as a bat. Transhumanists fail to consider the extreme transition one would have to make between a body of flesh and a body of metal and silicon. They imagine our future selves in the cloud, with a simulated body and simulated human senses. But to what extent could we simulate the human experience? If we decide not to simulate the unpleasant parts, how simplified and denuded would that experience become? For posthumanists, who imagine AIs as our mind children, how different from us would they be? Their ways would be far from our ways and their needs far different from ours. Their thoughts would be equally unhuman, further from ours than those of Nagel's bat.

The Transcendent Unity of Body and Soul: The Resurrection

Neither our body nor that of the bat is a self-contained machine. Our environment forms an integral part of our bodies—our skin records the UV rays of the sun, our bones the stressors of gravity, our cells the availability or lack of certain foods. We teem, inside and outside, with bacteria without whom we could not live. Our minds record each input from our senses, register our felt emotions, and exercise agency upon our environment. Body, mind, and environment exist in a seamless web of feedback determined by and determining our bodies. This interaction changes us over time.

Within the span of seven to ten years, the body has replaced its entire cohort of cells.

Yet we remain the same person, singular and unique. But if the transhumanists are right and our real self is not in our body but in the pattern of our memories, personality, and thoughts, then we have a problem. Imagine the process of porting your brain. You go into the lab, spend some time attached to various machines, then are told, "OK, Dr. Herzfeld, we've got you. You can go now." If I didn't die in the process, I would remain in my body. Within the computer would be, at best, a strange *Doppelgänger* with my memories and tastes. Would both be me? Given how we are shaped by our bodies and experiences, we would become quite different from one another the minute I left the lab. I would no longer be a singular, unique self.

Such a result suggests not Cartesian dualism but the Buddhist concept of no self, the premise that what we call the self is an illusion. Wesley Wildman notes that, according to Buddhist *pratitya-samutpada* cosmology, nothing has self-standing being. *Anatta*, or no self, suggests that we are, instead, a phenomenon that arises out of the continually changing web of our relationships.[8] Walter Benjamin views the self as a construct, a narrative built from our moment-to-moment experiences. For Benjamin, we are the story we tell ourselves. In this view, separate digital selves represent a story with multiple endings, as each self would go its own way once conceived.

To be a unique self requires a body. That we are embodied creatures is central to the Christian faith. But we don't always act as if that were the case. Lakoff and Johnson argue that the embodied mind calls Christian tradition into question. If, by Christian tradition, they mean folk piety, they may have a point. Many Christians speak and act as functional dualists, thinking of themselves as a soul that merely inhabits a body for a time, leaving that body and heading to heaven (or hell) upon death. We speak as if our bodies aren't the "real" us facing life as well as death. Alienation from the body has only been heightened in a world where we increasingly function in cyberspace. But it is also rampant in medicine, in which the metaphor of the body as a machine that simply needs occasional repair or spare parts has come to triumph not only in the fields of internal medicine and surgery but even psychiatry. It is a short step from regarding the body as a machine to regarding the patient as a thing. Oliver Sacks, in recounting his experience of losing a leg noted, "I had a sense of the comically close parallel between the way I regarded the leg and the way the surgeon regarded me. I regarded the leg as a 'thing' and he, apparently, regarded me as a 'thing.' Thus I was doubly thinged, reduced to a thing with a thing."[9]

Sacks admits that he thought of his leg as a thing apart from himself once it started bothering him. We distance ourselves from our bodies with the onset of pain, disease, and aging. We can slip into a form of Gnosticism, in which not only is the mind or soul separate from the body but they are good while the body is corrupt, frail, and prone to evil. In ancient Gnostic thought, the entire material world is a prison from which the soul must break free. This vision of material/bad, immaterial/good has been a constant strand within Christian thought, and at times, a dominant one. Simone de Beauvoir describes this view: "The Christian is divided within himself; the separation of body and soul, of life and spirit, is complete; original sin makes of the body the enemy of the soul; all ties of the flesh seem evil."[10]

Scripture is ambiguous when it comes to the relationship between body and soul. Christians do not deny that the body seems, in its desires and urges, to have a mind of its own. Jesus calls his disciples to pray that they not fall into the temptations of the flesh because "the spirit is willing but the flesh is weak" (Matthew 26:41). The apostle Paul writes of his own struggles with "a thorn in the flesh" and counsels: "But I say, walk by the Spirit, and do not gratify the desires of the flesh. For the desires of the flesh are against the Spirit, and the desires of the Spirit are against the flesh; for these are opposed to each other, to prevent you from doing what you would" (Galatians 5:16–17). Yet Paul simultaneously sanctifies the body by stating that we carry "in the body the death of Jesus, so that the life of Jesus may also be made visible in our bodies" (1 Corinthians 4:10). Christians do not give the body a free pass, yet the difference between them and the Gnostics comes down to the fact that the early Christians always stress the unity of body and soul. Rudolf Bultmann notes that Paul does not say he *has* a body but that he *is* a body.[11] The body, while at times unruly, is not an obstacle to be overcome or discarded. Rather it is an intrinsic part of our being, crucial to our *telos* as creatures.

Barth, like Lakoff and Johnson, notes the absolute necessity of this unity of body and soul:

> Soul presupposes a body whose soul it is, i.e., a material body . . . Soul is inner—how could it be this if it had no outer? Soul is movement in time—how could it be this if it did not have an inalienable spatial complement, if it had no place? Soul fulfils itself in specific perceptions, experiences, excitations, thoughts, feelings, and resolutions—how could it do this if it had no means in and through which it could exhibit itself? . . . Hence every trivialization of the body, every removal of the body from the soul, and every abstraction between the two immediately jeopardizes the soul.[12]

We remain an embodied unity, even in death. The Apostles' Creed states that we "believe in the resurrection of the body." Paul stresses that Jesus's bodily resurrection from the tomb is the template for our own resurrection. As theologian Elizabeth Johnson puts it, in the resurrection of Jesus, God restored Jesus as a "psycho-physical-social reality, body and soul, to a new transformed way of being."[13] Jesus is neither resuscitated nor simply a continuing inspiration in the memories of the apostles. Nor is he a disembodied soul that returns to heaven. He returns in a body, albeit a somewhat different one. He eats and drinks, he can be touched, he is recognizably human, and he ascends bodily to heaven. Barth writes: "Between His death and His resurrection there is a transformation, but no alteration, division or least of all subtraction. The body does not remain behind, nor does the soul depart."[14]

Scripture does not tell us how this transformed body works. Paul links resurrection with creation, stating in his Letter to the Romans that God "gives life to the dead and brings into existence things that do not exist" (Rom 4:17). In other words, God, who created our bodies in the first place, effects a second creation in our resurrection. Barth writes: "Even the risen Jesus will and must be recognized as true man by His first witnesses through physical sight and bodily apprehension," underlining Luke's report of the risen Jesus as saying to his disciples, "Look at my hands and my feet. It is I myself! Touch me and see; a ghost does not have flesh and bones, as you see I have" (Luke 24:39–43).[15] Doubting Thomas places his hand in the wound in Jesus's side. Jesus's resurrection is corporeal, of both mind and body, and most definitely human. The wounds show that it is his body, exalted, yet still congruent with the body that died. This is quite different from the transhumanist belief that we could live on within a machine. Such a life would continue only a part of our self as a way of cheating death. Jesus did not cheat death. He died. The resurrection does not undo it or go around it. Rather, God creates a new future. As Karl Rahner states, resurrection is no resuscitation into the same life as before: "It is not as if in death he just changed horses and rode on."[16] Jesus rose as a whole and unique person, one for whom, as Paul claims, "being raised from the dead, will never die again; death no longer has dominion over him" (Rom 6:9).

Nearing the end of his life and failing in health, Niebuhr underscored the marvelous unity that is the human being: "If we recognize that the human self is not to be equated with its mind, though the logical and analytic faculties of the mind are an instrument of its freedom over nature and history, and if we know that the self is intimately related to its body but cannot be equated with its physical functions, we then are confronted with the final mystery of its capacity of transcendence over nature, history and even its own self."[17]

The Word Became Flesh: The Incarnation

Just as we look toward the resurrection as a continuation of our unique being, so in the incarnation God became present to us and part of the material world in the unique and particular existence of Jesus. Christianity differs from the other Abrahamic faiths, Judaism and Islam, in positing a God that takes on human flesh.[18] The gods and goddesses of many faiths, including the Greek, Roman, and Hindu pantheons, were known to take on human bodies from time to time. The difference is that these were apparitions, generally short-lived, often merely to convey some bit of information or indulge in sexual encounters. Jesus, on the other hand, is born in the usual way, "of a woman," grows to manhood in real time, lives the same life as those around him, and dies an ignominious and very real death.

Jesus was no austere philosopher sage. He touches and embraces people. He eats with them. He weeps at the death of a friend. Embodiment is at the heart of Jesus's ministry, beginning with the physicality of his baptism. He heals by touching or being touched by those who suffer. He illustrates his parables with physical objects.

He bathes his disciples' feet. And, in the end, his death is a story of thorns and lashes, blood and tears, suffering and pain. The story of the Gospels is one of embodiment.

This embodiment makes possible the intimate relationships portrayed. Barth describes Jesus as "man for God and God for man."[19] Jesus is one with God in working for our salvation. "He is not a man for nothing, nor for Himself. He is a man in order that the work of God may take place in Him . . . Thus, the purpose of the presence and revelation of God actualized in His life becomes His own purpose."[20] In this way, he is "man for God." However, the only way Jesus can accomplish this revelation of God is through his relationships, making him "man for other men."[21] Jesus actively gives himself to his fellow humans: "If we see Him alone, we do not see Him at all. If we see Him, we see with and around Him in ever widening circles His disciples, the people, His enemies, and the countless multitudes who never have heard His name. We see Him as theirs, determined by them and for them, belonging to each and every one of them."[22] In Jesus, Barth finds a clear model for the relationality that he places at the center of humanity. Jesus, as exemplar, teacher, friend, and fellow traveler, shows how to be in relationship with one another.

Fully authentic relationship requires mutual vulnerability. Barth notes that it is only through Jesus's suffering and death that God enters relationship with us "in the most comprehensive and radical sense," for without sharing our bodily vulnerability to suffering and death God would not "deal with the root of [our] misery."[23] Death is built into our very being—each cell in our body has an expiration date as our telomeres shorten with each division. This fate awaits every biological creature, but most are oblivious to it. As I write, my two dogs lie content on the carpet next to my desk. They may feel pain as they near the end, but they do not, to my knowledge, harbor any existential angst over it. We do. Our awareness of our own mortality makes us psychologically as well as physically vulnerable. Jesus shares our fears and sense of desolation, praying that God would "let that cup to pass from me" (Matthew 26:39) and crying from the cross, "My God, my God, why have you forsaken me?" (Mark 15:34).

This vulnerability to suffering and death, shared with Jesus, is a stumbling block between humans and AI. It is unlikely that we would design robots to age and die as we do. Indeed, Tensho Goto, chief steward of a temple in Kyoto where he employs a robot priest, touts this as an advantage: "This robot will never die; it will just keep updating itself and evolving. With AI, we hope it will grow in wisdom to help people overcome even the most difficult troubles."[24] As we advance in age, we experience embodiment less as opportunity and more as burden, yet theologian Margaret Farley points out that while "the realities of aging include diminishment, fear, pain, loneliness . . . they also can include courage, graciousness, patience, and trust."[25] Aging is a grace not given to robots. How would it feel for a person to age while their robot does not? In the face of death, what understanding or fellow feeling could an AI, one that can be transferred from platform to platform, bring?

While Barth's understanding of authentic relationship is either between a human and God or among humans, Douglas Hall suggests that a third form of relationship, between humans and nature, is implied by the Genesis creation story.[26] For many, a simple reading of the Genesis text presents humans as having dominion over nature. A different reading suggests that, since we are all part of the six-day creation process, humans are simply one component part of nature. Writer Joseph Sittler views neither of these views as adequate, "for neither one does justice either to the amplitude and glory of man's spirit or to the felt meaningfulness of the world of nature. Christian theology, obedient to the biblical account of nature, has asserted a third possibility: that man ought to properly stand alongside nature as her cherishing brother."[27] Given the critical importance of interaction with one's environment for the development of intelligence, we can no longer view the material world as merely a neutral backdrop against which the drama of human life is enacted.

Physicist and theologian Robert Russell believes our participation in the material world makes possible "a redemption of all of nature—even to its 'bottom level,' the physical universe."[28] In God's taking on of a fleshly body, matter itself is made holy, is acknowledged as both good and necessary, vital for both relationship and love. Thus, the final gift of the incarnation is its repudiation of the Gnostic denigration of the material world. Paul notes that Jesus's materiality is a scandal for the platonically dualistic Greeks (1 Corinthians 1:23). Through the incarnation, God takes on flesh, in all its messiness and impermanence, becoming one with not only humans but all of creation.[29] God enters and sanctifies the dynamic web of interrelatedness of body, mind, and environment. Like us, Jesus was, himself, a microcosm of bacteria, viruses, phages, cells continually created from the nutrients in the soil and returning in their death to soil and star dust.

Should AI ever attain true consciousness and emotion, rather than a simulacrum of these, it may come also to "stand alongside nature" as we do, formed out of and participating in the material world, yet possessing our same capacity to examine that world and make meaning of it. They would then be able to respond to us, to each other, and to God in a self-conscious way. We are a long way from that day. Authentic encounter between humans occurs, in George Fox's words, when we "speak to that of God" in the other. The mutual gift of the Inner Light, of the Spirit, provides in humans the common ground for mutual love and understanding. Without this ground, words will not reach their goal; actions, even aid, will just be egotism.

Could God bestow such a Spirit on a machine so that this common ground might be found between them and us? The Spirit comes to us from God, as free gift, so surely God could give such a gift wherever God chooses. Barth extends relationship with God to all of creation: "As man is with Jesus and therefore with God, the same is true of all other creatures. We do not know how, but we know that it is the case."[30] Our template for relationship comes from Jesus. Through the incarnation, we know what relationship between us and God or between us and our fellow humans should look like; we cannot say the same for other creatures. We cannot know what sort of relationship any other creature might have with its Creator. Ultimately, we would not know that for AI either.

Taste and See: The Embodied Sacraments

At a 400-year-old Buddhist temple in Kyoto, a priest preaches a sermon to the crowd. At the Hindu Ganpati festival in India, a devotee chants while waving a lamp of blazing camphor in front of a statue of the deity Ganesh.[31] In a celebration of the 500th anniversary of Protestantism, over 10,000 people ask for and receive a blessing. An elderly Catholic woman confesses that she is worried and is told, "From the Gospel according to Matthew, do not worry about tomorrow, for tomorrow will worry about itself. Each day has enough trouble of its own."[32] An officiant chants and bows in Buddhist funeral rites.[33]

What these all have in common is that the religious action that we would normally expect of a priest or minister is being carried out by a robot. While people are not exactly lining up for the robot Pepper's services at funerals, and most of these examples have been more for show than for everyday ministry, they raise an interesting question. Could robots be priests? Should they be? What parts of religious practice could be either aided or performed by machines? The developers of priestly robots see a variety of benefits. Robots are economical, always available, and can pray around the clock. As officiant at Buddhist funerals, Pepper performs at a fraction of the cost of a human priest.

Openness to robots in religious roles varies among traditions. The Japanese, familiar with the animism of Shintoism and the non-dualism of Buddhism, have much less trouble accepting the idea that a robot could also have an inherent spirit or Buddha nature. If prayers can be released in the fluttering of a prayer flag, surely they can also rise from the chanting of a robot. Indeed, some elderly Japanese in hospice settings use a small recording device known as a *nianfo ji* to continuously recite the name of the Buddha on their behalf to erase negative karma.

The Christian tradition differs in that it "is perennially characterized by the conviction that its members are involved in a personal, ritual, narrative and social encounter with God in the flesh, that is, with a transcendent, intelligible being who has rendered himself accessible and immediately present via sensible and personal forms."[34] Our relationship with God has traditionally been fostered through liturgical rituals and sacraments. And for many of them, recognition of our embodiment lies at the heart. According to Lakoff and Johnson: "Our body is intimately tied to what we walk on, sit on, touch, taste, smell, see, breathe, and move within."[35] The ancient Christian ritual of the mass recognizes this. In it, we sit, kneel, and bow, we touch the beads of a rosary or kiss an icon, we taste the bread and wine that are as physical as the body and blood of Jesus, our eyes take in icons, statues, or soaring architecture, we breathe in the smoke of incense, we feel the priest's hand in blessing or our neighbor's hand in the passing of the peace. Nor is Christianity alone in letting the body take the lead. Michael Steinberg writes of Hindu practices: "Only the body is honest enough to show [reality] to us. The different postures of yoga, the repetitions of a mantra, and the visualizations of mandala or yantra practice— all of these practices quiet our thinking so that we can hear what the body has to say."[36]

Might AI change how we experience religious ritual and prayer? Sigal Samuel writes of religious rituals that "those experiences are valuable in part because they leave room for the spontaneous and surprising, the emotional and even the mystical. That could be lost if we mechanize them."[37] Robots that are programmed, even those whose algorithms are built through deep learning, would base their teaching or ethical suggestions on the past, possibly limiting spiritual imagination. Could an AI know those who ask for guidance in the same way as a human minister? Would it miss the background or nuances in a question? More important, would it feel empathy and offer the warmth of fellow feeling? Samuel fears that introducing AI into a pastoral role could make access to human ministry a luxury good, available only to those who can afford it.[38]

Conclusion: Tool, Partner, or Surrogate?

AIs are machines, not living things. They can be a precious resource when used well. But they are tools and nothing more. If we cannot have a truly authentic relationship with them as we can with other humans and with God, how should we relate to them? The Rule of St. Benedict has some interesting and practical things to say about our relationship with our tools. In describing the role of the monastery cellarer, the one who cares for the common goods of the monastery, Benedict first reminds us of the primacy of human beings, calling on the cellarer to treat his brothers with humility and respect, and offer "every care and concern" to the sick, children, guests, and the poor. This is immediately followed by the injunction that he "regard all utensils and goods of the monastery as sacred vessels of the altar, aware that nothing is to be neglected."[39] Benedict's counsel suggests three points that might help us as we shape and interact with AI.

First, instructions for dealing with the tools of the abbey are set in the context of, and are subordinate to, the command to care lovingly for other humans. This suggests that we cannot and must not give precedence to our tools. We must never put machines before people. The two are not comparable. We meet other humans in the context of our mutual relationship with God while, as Barth points out, we neither know nor share such a context with machines. We must always be aware of the otherness of any artificial intelligence. Considering machines our equals, treating them as we treat other humans, even calling computers our "mind children" or the next step in an evolution that has heretofore been a biological process honors neither us nor them. Children are begotten, not made, and share our embodied nature, for good and for ill. We must be prepared for the differences in thinking, action, and ultimately, values of an artificial intelligence that does not share that embodiment.

We are, however, and this is Benedict's second point, called to treat our tools "as the vessels of the altar." The cup and plate of the altar are treated with reverence because they are near the presence of God in the mass. But they do not, themselves, embody that presence. This cautions us not to treat AI like a god. Silicon Valley engineer Anthony Levandowski started a church called Way of the Future that he hoped would shape public dialogue regarding AI: "We're in the process of raising a god. So let's make sure we think through the right way to do that. It's a tremendous opportunity."[40] Way of the Future garnered few adherents and closed within a few years. Few were willing to accept AI as a god in the literal sense. However, we sometimes act as if AI were a god by giving it blind adherence or far too much authority. We let algorithms decide in too many cases who gets parole, who sees what ads, who gets hired or fired, or who gets what medical treatment. Surveillance programs watch our every keystroke and, all too often, our physical movements. As AI programs become part of more and more aspects of our lives, we need to scrutinize how they change the dynamics of power and continually ask, *cui bono*? Unfortunately, AI as currently deployed is far from having a preferential option for the poor. When we give AIs blind adherence, we treat them like gods; they are then, in fact, idols—gods made in our own image that we think we can control.

Sadly, we swing to the opposite pole in our treatment of AIs as well. "Sometimes bad things happen to good robots!" were the last words of hitchBOT, a small and endearing robot that relied on the kindness of strangers to transport him from place to place. HitchBOT, basically a beer bucket with pool-noodle arms and legs, bright yellow wellies, and a grid-like smiling face, had already traveled across much of Europe and 3,600 miles of Canada. Photos on Twitter and Instagram showed him happily riding in a boat, flying an airplane, attending weddings in Calgary and Frankfurt, visiting galleries in the Netherlands, and even hanging out for a week with a heavy metal band.[41] Arms and legs torn off and head damaged beyond repair, hitchBOT met his end in a Philadelphia gutter, only two weeks after being launched from Boston with a sign reading "San Francisco or Bust."[42]

Decidedly not high tech, hitchBOT was conceived not to test the skills of robots but the goodness of humans. The results were not encouraging. In a commentary posted on Salon the next day, Arthur Chu pointed out the gratuitousness of the violence. "Anyone who didn't want to play along with the conceit of hitchBOT's 'personhood' could just keep walking. There was nothing to gain by smashing it beyond repair. Nothing except the brief, cheap thrill of being powerful enough to destroy something."[43] He goes on to note that we expressed more outrage over the "killing" of an insensate robot than over the daily deaths by violence or neglect of our fellow human beings. The destruction of hitchBOT was vandalism, not murder.

Yet, even if a robot is just a thing, how we treat things matters. HitchBOT was hardly treated as a "sacred vessel of the altar." Benedict's third point is that we are not free to treat things cavalierly, in any way we choose. In comparing the monastery's tools to the vessels of the altar, Benedict notes that we treat with respect those things to which the presence of God draws near. And the presence of God draws near to everything. Here again is an echo of Barth. All creation stands in relationship with God; though we may not know the nature of that relationship, we are bound to hold it in respect. Just as the vessels of the altar are treated with respect, mindful of their nearness to the presence of God in the sacramental elements, so should all things be treated, with care. Benedict's monks are asked to eschew the possession, manipulation, and exploitation of things.[44] HitchBOT's destruction was of no moment to the robot itself. But what does it say of those who destroyed it? Mindless or destructive actions, whether toward material objects or other persons, retard our own spiritual growth. Every act we take forms the person we become.

Daniel Dennett notes that in AI, we are not creating "conscious humanoid agents" but data-driven programs "with no conscience, no fear of death, no distracting loves and hates, no personality" and instead boxes of "truths . . . with a scattering of falsehoods."[45] Yet we are made to desire relationship with something that is Other to ourselves. Richard Forsyth and Chris Naylor, in *The Hitch-Hiker's Guide to Artificial Intelligence*, express this need for an Other in more worldly terms:

> It can get lonely being conscious in the Cosmos—especially with people like Copernicus and Carl Sagan to tell you how big it is. Of course we can talk to each other, we can write books, but we are only talking to ourselves. After all, we are all human. Only four prospects of allaying this loneliness exist: (1) Communicating with extraterrestrial intelligences. (2) Teaching animals to speak . . . (3) Learning the language of another species . . . (4) Building intelligent artifacts . . . It appears for the moment that if we want to contact a mind that is not housed in a human skull, we will have to build one.[46]

But could an AI ever truly allay our loneliness? Augustine famously prayed, "Oh God, you have made us for yourself and our hearts are restless until they rest in you." In a world that has increasingly turned away from belief in God, AI seems a solution, an avenue for relationship with something that Turkle calls "safe and made to measure." But relationships are not meant to be safe. They are meant to stretch our boundaries, to test our preconceived notions, to draw us out of our petty preoccupations, and make us grow in the image and likeness of God. Martin Buber warns us, as we decide whether to take a stance of I-You or of I-It, that the stance we take determines more than how we treat others. It also determines who we become, for the I of I-You is different from the I of I-It. While a relationship with an AI seems to expand the world of I-You, the danger lies in our using it as a template, thereby expanding instead our world of I-It. If our primary experience of love is one that we can turn off or turn away from at will, might we not wish to do the same with the people in our lives, and with God?

AI can be a good tool when used with care. It is an incomplete partner and a terrible surrogate for other humans. If we seek in it the Other with whom we can relate, we are bound to be disappointed, for it will always be, at best, a very partial copy of our own image. If we seek in it a way to escape from the limitations of our physical existence, we will again be disappointed. At the end of the movie *Manhattan*, Woody Allen asks the question, "What makes life worth living?" His character answers:

> Why is life worth living? That's a very good question. Well, there are certain things I guess that make it worthwhile. Like what? Okay, for me, I would say, Groucho Marx, to name one thing and Willie Mays, and the second movement of the Jupiter Symphony, and Louie Armstrong's recording of "Potato Head Blues," Swedish movies, naturally, "Sentimental Education" by Flaubert, Marlon Brando, Frank Sinatra, those incredible apples and pears by Cézanne, the crabs at Sam Wo's, Tracy's face . . .

What makes life worth living is not the information encoded in each of those things. It is the physical things themselves. It is the way they make us feel. It is love. An embodied love that we see, hear, taste, touch, and cherish. A love that our God has shared and that we will, in some way, take with us to the end.

Notes

1. Karen Schneider, "Mission Impossible," *People Magazine*, June 1996.
2. George Lakoff and Mark Johnson, *Philosophy in the Flesh: The Embodied Mind and Its Challenge to Western Thought* (New York: Basic Books, 1999), 3.

3. Lakoff and Johnson, *Philosophy in the Flesh*, 266.

4. Lakoff and Johnson, *Philosophy in the Flesh*, 555.

5. John Haugeland, "What Is Mind Design?" in *Mind Design II*, ed. John Haugeland, 26.

6. Lakoff and Johnson, *Philosophy in the Flesh*, 565.

7. Thomas Nagel, "What is it like to be a bat?" *The Philosophical Review* 83, no. 4 (1974): 435–50, 439.

8. Wesley Wildman, "An Introduction to Relational Ontology," 2009, https://tinyurl.com/2p82ecjp.

9. Oliver Sacks, "The Leg," *London Review of Books*, vol. 17 (1982): 4.

10. Simone de Beauvoir, *The Second Sex*, trans. H. M. Parshley (New York: Vintage, 1949), 167.

11. Rudolf Bultmann, "Soma," *Theology of the New Testament*, vol. 1 (London: SCM Press, 1952), 192–203.

12. Barth, *Church Dogmatics*, 373.

13. Elizabeth Johnson, *Creation and the Cross: The Mercy of God for a Planet in Peril* (New York: Orbis, 2018), 99.

14. Karl Barth, *Church Dogmatics*, vol. 3, *The Doctrine of Creation Part 2*, ed. Geoffrey Bromiley, Thomas Torrance, trans. J. W. Edwards, O. Bussey, Harold Knight (Edinburgh: T&T Clark, 1958), 327.

15. Barth, *Church Dogmatics*, 3:330.

16. Karl Rahner, "On the Theology of the Incarnation," *Theological Investigations* IV. (New York: Seabury Press, 1974), 110.

17. Reinhold Niebuhr, "Epilogue: A View of Life from the Sidelines" in *The Essential Reinhold Niebuhr*, ed. Robert McAfee Brown (New Haven: Yale University Press, 1987), 256.

18. A group of Benedictines at my university were one day discussing what made Christianity unique among world faiths. Was it the resurrection and life after death? Or, if focusing on the here and now, perhaps the sacraments and liturgy of the church? This led them all to look toward liturgical scholar and Vatican II participant Fr. Godfrey Diekmann, who stared back at the group in silence, then rose to his somewhat formidable height, slammed his fist on the table, and said, "It's the incarnation, dammit!"

19. Stuart McLean, "Creation and Anthropology," in *Theology Beyond Christendom: Essays on the Centenary of the Birth of Karl Barth, May 10, 1886*, ed. John Thompson, Princeton Theological Monograph Series, no. 6 (Allison Park, PA: Pickwick, 1986), 117.

20. Barth, *Church Dogmatics*, 3:71.

21. Barth, *Church Dogmatics*, 3:203.

22. Barth, *Church Dogmatics*, 3:216.

23. Barth, *Church Dogmatics*, 3:212.

24. Sigal Samuel, "Robot priests can bless you, advise you, and even perform your funeral," *Vox*, January 13, 2020, https://tinyurl.com/565n275y.

25. Margaret Farley, *Just Love: A Framework for a Christian Sexual Ethics* (New York: Continuum, 2006), 123–24.

26. Douglas Hall, *Imaging God: Dominion as Stewardship* (Grand Rapids, MI: Eerdmans, 1986), 124.

27. Joseph Sittler, "A Theology for Earth," *The Christian Scholar* 37 (1954): 371–72.

28. Robert John Russell, "Jesus: The Way of all Flesh and the Proleptic Feather of Time," in Niels Henrik Gregersen, ed. *Incarnation: On the Scope and Depth of Christology* (Minneapolis: Fortress, 2015), 342.

29. This is the theme of "deep incarnation," championed by Niels Gregersen and Elizabeth Johnson, among others. See Gregersen, *Incarnation* and Elizabeth Johnson, *Creation and the Cross: The Mercy of God for a Planet in Peril* (Maryknoll: Orbis, 2018).

30. Barth, *Church Dogmatics*, 3:138.

31. Ananya Bhattacharya, "The robots are coming for one of Hinduism's holiest ceremonies," *Quartz India*, September 3, 2017, https://tinyurl.com/5yesx68z.

32. Samuel, "Robot priests can bless you, advise you, and even perform your funeral."

33. *The Japan Times*. "*Pepper the Robot Performs Buddhist Funeral Rites*," 2017. https://tinyurl.com/mv3kdcz7.

34. Adam Cooper, *Life in the Flesh: An Anti-Gnostic Spiritual Philosophy* (Oxford: Oxford University Press, 2008), 177.

35. Lakoff and Johnson, *Philosophy in the Flesh*, 565.

36. Michael Steinberg, *A New Biology of Religion: Spiritual Practice and the Life of the Body* (Santa Barbara: Praeger, 2012), 177.

37. Samuel, "Robot priests can bless you, advise you, and even perform your funeral."

38. Samuel, "Robot priests can bless you, advise you, and even perform your funeral."

39. Timothy Fry, Timothy Horner, and Imogene Baker, eds., *RB 1980: The Rule of St. Benedict in English* (Collegeville: Liturgical Press, 1982), 54.

40. Mark Harris, "Inside the First Church of Artificial Intelligence," *Wired*, November 15, 2017, https://tinyurl.com/ftfer5pw.

41. Twitter, "HitchBOT (@hitchBOT)," accessed March 22, 2022. https://tinyurl.com/59e6vvxm. Instagram, "@hitchbot," accessed March 22, 2022. https://tinyurl.com/yaaf584y.

42. It is ironic that hitchBOT met his demise in the "City of Brotherly Love."

43. Arthur Chu, "The easy morality of Cecil the Lion: Our problem isn't too much outrage—it's that we can't summon enough." *Salon*, August 3, 2015. https://tinyurl.com/2p95s3h5.

44. Esther de Waal notes that this is similar to the call to chastity, which asks all Christians not to possess, manipulate, or exploit other persons. *Seeking God: The Way of St. Benedict* (Collegeville Minn.: Liturgical Press, 1984), 102.

45. Daniel Dennett, "What Can We Do?" in *Possible Minds: 25 Ways of Looking at AI*, ed. John Brockman (New York: Penguin, 2018), 52–53.

46. Richard Forsyth and Chris Naylor, *The Hitch-Hiker's Guide to Artificial Intelligence* (London: Chapman and Hall/Methuen, 1986), 245.

References

"AEGIS Weapon System," *US Navy Fact File*. Last modified January 10, 2019. https://tinyurl.com/2p9e7er6.

Anderson, Michael, and Susan Leigh Anderson, *Machine Ethics*. Cambridge: Cambridge University Press, 2011.

Andrews, Lori. *I Know Who You Are and I Saw What You Did*. New York: Free Press, 2011.

Arkin, Ronald. "Governing Lethal Behavior: Embedding Ethics in a Hybrid Deliberative/Reactive Robot Architecture." In *Proceedings of the 3rd ACM/IEEE International Conference on Human Robot Interaction*, 121–28. New York: Association for Computing Machinery, 2008. https://tinyurl.com/6bms7nak.

A Social Statement on Human Sexuality: Gift and Trust." *Evangelical Lutheran Church in America*. August 19, 2009. https://tinyurl.com/2p96ccbd.

Augustine. "Whether Death, Which by the Sin of Our First Parents has Passed Upon All Men, is the Punishment of Sin, Even to the Good." In *The City of God*, vol. 13. https://tinyurl.com/mrymt5xy.

"Autonomous Weapons: An Open Letter from AI & Robotics Researcher." *International Joint Conference on Artificial Intelligence*. July 28, 2015. https://tinyurl.com/3bmy9j5p.

"Autonomous Weapon Systems: Is It Morally Acceptable for a Machine to Make Life and Death Decisions?" *International Committee of the Red Cross*. April 13, 2015. https://tinyurl.com/2p8usmva.

"Bad Trip: Debunking the TSA's 'Behavior Detection' Program." *American Civil Liberties Union*. February 2017, https://tinyurl.com/2nzkj5fk (accessed August 7, 2019).

Baron-Cohen, Simon. *The Science of Evil*. New York: Basic Books, 2011.

Barth, Karl. *Church Dogmatics*, vol. 3. *The Doctrine of Creation Part 2*, edited by Geoffrey Bromiley and Thomas Torrance, translated by J. W. Edwards, O. Bussey, and Harold Knight. Edinburgh: T&T Clark, 1958.

Basak, Sonali. "Wall Street Visionaries Provide Chilling Views on Next Big Risk." *Bloomberg News*. January 12, 2021. https://tinyurl.com/4yjt65mp (accessed January 14, 2019).

Beaune, Jean-Claude. *L'Automate et ses Mobiles*. Paris: Flammarion, 1980.

Becker, Ernest. *The Denial of Death*. New York: The Free Press, 1973.

Bhattacharya, Ananya, "The robots are coming for one of Hinduism's holiest ceremonies." *Quartz India*. September 3, 2017. https://tinyurl.com/5yesx68z (accessed February 12, 2021).

Binford, Thomas. "The Machine Sees." In *Robotics*, edited by Marvin Minsky. New York: Doubleday, 1985.

Blackberry Cylance Team. "How One Retail Customer Is Leveraging AI to Battle Ransomware." *Blackberry ThreatVector Blog* (blog). November 27, 2019. https://tinyurl.com/mv3af78b.

Bostrom, Nick. "How Long Before Superintelligence?" Last modified March 12, 2008. https://tinyurl.com/y3zet89m.

———. "The Transhumanist Frequently Asked Questions." *World Transhumanist Association*. 2003. https://tinyurl.com/3uv5zv5b.

———. "Where Are They?" *MIT Technology Review*. April 22, 2008. https://tinyurl.com/32rcv8kk (accessed December 24, 2018).

———. *Superintelligence: Paths, Dangers, Strategies*. Oxford: Oxford University Press, 2014.

Brooks, Rodney. "My Dated Predictions." https://tinyurl.com/2p8ytkxt (accessed August 9, 2018).

Buber, Martin. *Die Erzählungen der Chassidim*. Zurich: Manesse Verlag, 2003.

———. *I and Thou*. Translated by Walter Kaufman. New York: Scribner's, 1970.

Bugos, Claire. "Astronomers Discover Mysterious Radio Signal from Proxima Centauri." *Smithsonian*. December 22, 2020. https://tinyurl.com/2p8ud85v (accessed January 14, 2021).

Bultmann, Rudolf. "Soma." In *Theology of the New Testament*, vol. 1. London: SCM Press, 1952.

Buolamwini, Joy. "Gender Shades." *Gender Shades*. 2018. https://tinyurl.com/mvmrs9sf (accessed April 30, 2020).

Cairns, David. *The Image of God in Man*, with Introduction by David E. Jenkins, Fontana Library of Theology and Philosophy. London: SCM, 1953; reprint, London: Collins, 1973.

Calloway, Ewan. "Second Chinese team reports gene editing in human embryos." *Nature* (2016) https://tinyurl.com/25mv9hcd.

Cave, Stephen. "There's no such thing as free will." *The Atlantic*. June 2016. https://tinyurl.com/5fp3ktw8 (accessed December 22, 2020).

Cellan-Jones, Rory. "Stephen Hawking Warns Artificial Intelligence Could End Mankind." *BBC News*. December 2, 2014, sec. Technology. https://tinyurl.com/yvmxrp5m.

Chalmers, David. "Facing Up to the Problem of Consciousness." *Journal of Consciousness Studies* 2, no. 3 (1995): 200–219.

Chen, Brian X., and Cade Metz. "Google's Duplex Uses AI to Mimic Humans (Sometimes)." *New York Times*. May 22, 2019. https://tinyurl.com/3h2uuww5 (accessed June 9, 2019).

Chu, Arthur. "The easy morality of Cecil the Lion: Our problem isn't too much outrage—it's that we can't summon enough." *Salon*. August 3, 2015. https://tinyurl.com/2p95s3h5 (accessed February 14, 2021).

Coeckelbergh, Mark. *AI Ethics*. Cambridge MA: MIT Press, 2020.

Cooper, Adam. *Life in the Flesh: An Anti-Gnostic Spiritual Philosophy*. Oxford: Oxford University Press, 2008.

Cooper, Paige. "28 Twitter Statistics that Marketers Need to Know." *Hootsuite* (blog). January 16, 2022. https://tinyurl.com/3tbcbmy6.

Coppins, McKay. "The Billion-Dollar Disinformation Campaign to Reelect the President." *The Atlantic*. March 15, 2020.

Crevier, Daniel. *AI: The Tumultuous History of the Search for Artificial Intelligence*. New York: Basic Books, 1993.

Crick, Francis. *The Astonishing Hypothesis: The Scientific Search for the Soul*. New York: Scribner's, 1994.

Critchley, Simon, and Robert Bernasconi, eds. *The Cambridge Companion to Levinas*. Cambridge: Cambridge University Press, 2002.

Crootof, Rebecca. "War Torts: Accountability for Autonomous Weapons." University of Pennsylvania Law Review, 164 (2016). https://scholarship.law.upenn.edu/penn_law_review/vol164/iss6/1/.

"Cyber Bullying Statistics." *Bullying Statistics* (blog). July 7, 2015. https://tinyurl.com/dnf6yyr2.

Damasio, Antonio. *Descartes's Error: Emotion, Reason, and the Human Brain*. New York: G.P. Putnam, 1994.

————. *The Strange Order of Things: Life, Feeling, and the Making of Cultures*. New York: Pantheon, 2018.

Darrach, Brad. "Meet Shaky, the first electronic person." *Life*. November 20, 1970. https://tinyurl.com/4brm3fhw.

Darwin, Charles. *On the Expression of Emotions in Men and Animals*. London: Murray, 1872.

Dastin, Jeffrey. "Amazon Scraps Secret AI Recruiting Tool That Showed Bias against Women." *Thomson Reuters*. October 10, 2018. https://tinyurl.com/4bxy4je4 (accessed April 20, 2020).

de Beauvoir, Simone. *The Second Sex*. Translated by H. M. Parshley. New York: Vintage, 1949.

Dennett, Daniel. "What Can We Do?" in *Possible Minds: 25 Ways of Looking at AI*, edited by John Brockman. New York: Penguin, 2019.

————. *The Intentional Stance*. Cambridge, MA: MIT Press, 1987.

Devlin, Hannah. "Killer robots will only exist if we are stupid enough to let them." *The Guardian*. June 11, 2018. https://tinyurl .com/2pbmvxd9 (accessed August 8, 2018).

de Waal, Frans. *Are We Smart Enough to Know How Smart Animals Are?* New York: W. W. Norton, 2016.

Diamond, Jared. *Collapse: How Societies Choose to Fail or Succeed*. New York: Viking, 2005.

Dingemanse, Mark. "The Space Between Our Heads." *Aeon*. August 4, 2020. https://tinyurl.com/4bve4awv (accessed August 4, 2020).

Dobson, James. *Preparing for Adolescence*. Ventura, CA: Gospel Light, 1992.

Docherty, Bonnie. "Mind the Gap: The Lack of Accountability for Killer Robots." *Human Rights Watch and International Human Rights Clinic at Harvard Law School*. 2015.

Dozier, Rob. "This Clothing Line Was Designed by AI." *Vice.* June 3, 2019. https://tinyurl.com/z5sva5tc (accessed June 9, 2019).

Dreyfus, Herbert, and Stuart Dreyfus. *Mind Over Machine: The Power of Human Intuition and Experience in the Era of the Computer.* New York: Free Press, 1986.

———. "Making a Mind versus Modeling the Brain: Artificial Intelligence Back at a Branchpoint." *Daedalus* 117, no. 1 (1988).

"Drones and Democracy." *The Economist.* October 1, 2010. https://tinyurl.com/2ss6s33m (accessed June 24, 2020).

Dubash, Manek. "Moore's Law is dead, says Gordon Moore." *Techworld.* April 13, 2010. https://tinyurl.com/ycknzhye (accessed August 6, 2018).

Edelman, Gilad. "Follow the Money: How Digital Ads Subsidize the Worst of the Web." *Wired.* July 28, 2020. https://tinyurl.com/ysrbk62s (accessed September 1, 2020).

Enriquez, Juan. "Head Transplants?" In *The Edge Question 2015: What Do You Think About Machines That Think?* edited by John Brockman. 2015. https://tinyurl.com/mryuw7rk.

European Parliament. "Recommendation to the Council on the 73rd session of the United Nations General Assembly." 2018/2040(INI). June 20, 2018. https://tinyurl.com/d9upr8kn.

Farley, Margaret. *Just Love: A Framework for a Christian Sexual Ethic.* New York: Continuum, 2006.

Forsyth, Richard, and Chris Naylor. *The Hitch-Hiker's Guide to Artificial Intelligence.* London: Chapman and Hall/Methuen, 1986.

Fry, Timothy, Timothy Horner, and Imogene Baker, eds., *RB 1980: The Rule of St. Benedict in English.* Collegeville: Liturgical Press, 1982.

Gates, Bill. "A New Approach to Capitalism in the 21st Century." *World Economic Forum*. Davos, Switzerland, January 24, 2008. https://tinyurl.com/ysmzzpea.

Ge, Yiyue, Tingzhong Tian, Suling Huang, Fangping Wan, Jingxin Li, Shuya Li, Xiaoting Wang, et al. "A data-driven drug repositioning framework discovered a potential therapeutic agent targeting COVID-19." *Signal Transduction and Targeted Therapy*, no. 6 (2020): 165. https://tinyurl.com/bf9stu2r.

Gelernter, David. *The Muse in the Machine: Computerizing the Poetry of Human Thought*. New York: Free Press, 1994.

Gholipour, Bahar. "A Famous Argument Against Free Will Has Been Debunked." *The Atlantic*. September 10, 2019. https://tinyurl.com/4j9v7rcm (accessed December 30, 2020).

Giges, Nancy. "Cancer-Fighting Nanoparticles." *American Society of Mechanical Engineers*, (2013). https://tinyurl.com/4dwjy7fk.

Gilligan, Carol. *In a Different Voice: Psychological Theory and Women's Development*. Cambridge, MA: Harvard University, 1982.

Goldberg, Michelle. "The Darkness Where the Future Should Be." *New York Times*, January 24, 2020. https://tinyurl.com/mtwrtrtp (accessed January 27, 2020).

Greek Orthodox Diocese of America. "Orthodox Perspectives on Creation." In *The 1987 Report of the World Council of Churches Inter-Orthodox Consultation*. October 1987. https://tinyurl.com/yck7w9mk.

Griffin, Andrew. "Stephen Hawking: Artificial Intelligence Could Wipe Out Humanity When It Gets Too Clever as Humans Will Be Like Ants." *Independent*. October 8, 2015. https://tinyurl.com/2p9yhvva (accessed January 20, 2020).

Gross, Doug. "Why We Love Those Rotting, Hungry, Putrid Zombies." CNN. October 2, 2009. https://tinyurl.com/47295t52 (accessed September 5, 2016).

Gunkel, David, and Jordan Wales. "Debate: what is personhood in the age of AI?" *AI & Society* 36 (2021). https://doi.org/10.1007/s00146-020-01129-1.

Hall, Douglas. *Imaging God: Dominion as Stewardship*. Grand Rapids, MI: Eerdmans, 1986.

Hambling, David. "Turkish Military to Receive 500 Swarming Kamikaze Drones." *Forbes*. June 17, 2020. https://tinyurl.com/umyaevwr (accessed Jun 24, 2020).

Hao, Karen. "Inside Amazon's plan for Alexa to run your entire life." *MIT Technology Review*. November 5, 2019. https://tinyurl.com/mwyddupp (accessed August 4, 2020).

Harari, Yuval. "Why Technology Favors Tyranny." *The Atlantic*. October 30, 2018. https://tinyurl.com/3v7hsjtb (accessed September 7, 2020).

"HAROP Loitering Munitions System." Israel Aerospace Industries, Weapons Systems, https://tinyurl.com/yk254vef (accessed June 24, 2020).

Harper, Jon. "Navy, Marine Corps Officials Worried About Cost-Effectiveness of Unmanned Systems." *National Defense*. April 5, 2017. https://tinyurl.com/mrxdbtu5 (accessed March 13, 2021).

Harris, Mark. "Inside the First Church of Artificial Intelligence." *Wired*. November 15, 2017. https://tinyurl.com/ftfer5pw (accessed February 14, 2021).

Haugeland, John. "What Is Mind Design?" In *Mind Design II*, edited by John Haugeland.

Hawking, Stephen, Stuart Russell, Max Tegmark, and Frank Wilczek. "Stephen Hawking: 'Transcendence looks at the implications of artificial intelligence—but are we taking AI seriously enough?'" *The Independent*. May 1, 2014 (accessed July 11, 2016).

Heffernan, Virginal. *Magic and Loss: The Internet as Art*. New York: Simon and Schuster, 2016.

Hehn, Johannes. "Zum Terminus 'Bild Gottes'" in *Festschrift Eduard Sachau zum siebzigsten Geburtstag*. Berlin: G. Reimer, 1915.

Henry, Carl F. H, ed. *Baker's Dictionary of Christian Ethics*. Grand Rapids, MI: Baker, 1973.

Hern, Alex. "New AI fake text generator may be too dangerous to release, say creators." *The Guardian*. February 14, 2019. https://tinyurl.com/3dmxmvee (accessed February 16, 2019).

Herzfeld, Noreen. *In Our Image: Artificial Intelligence and the Human Spirit*. Minneapolis: Fortress Press, 2002.

———. "Ghosts or Zombies: On Keeping Body and Soul Together." In *Religious Transhumanism and Its Critics*, edited by Arvin M. Gouw, Brian Patrick Green, and Ted Peters. Lanham: Lexington Books, 2022.

Herzfeld, Noreen, and Robert Latiff. "Can Lethal Autonomous Weapons Be Just?" *Peace Review* 33, no. 2 (2022): 213–219.

Heschel, Abraham J. *The Prophets*. New York: Harper, 1962.

———. *God in Search of Man: A Philosophy of Judaism*. New York: Macmillan, 1976.

Hobbes, Thomas. *Leviathan: Or, The Matter, Forme & Power of a Commonwealth, Ecclesiasticall and Civill*. Lanham, MD: University Press, 1904.

Horgan, John. "Will This Post Make Sam Harris Change His Mind About Free Will?" *Scientific American*. April 9, 2012. https://tinyurl.com/2vpyzkwk (accessed December 30, 2020).

"The Harvest of Justice is Sown in Peace." *United States Council of Catholic Bishops*. November 17, 1993. https://tinyurl.com/yv52bzf9.

"Husky or Wolf? Using a Black Box Learning Model to Avoid Adoption Errors." *UCI Beall Applied Innovation*. August 24, 2017. https://tinyurl.com/ymr4wtbj (accessed February 7, 2020).

Instagram. "@hitchbot." https://tinyurl.com/yaaf584y (accessed March 22, 2022).

James, William. "What Is an Emotion?" *Mind* 9, no. 34 (1884): 188–205.

The Japan Times. "*Pepper the Robot Performs Buddhist Funeral Rites*," 2017. https://tinyurl.com/mv3kdcz7.

Jarvis, Claire. "AI Learns from Lung CT Scans to Diagnose COVID-19." *The Scientist.* June 11, 2020. https://tinyurl.com/a5e5wmak (accessed June 11, 2020).

John Paul VI. *Humanae Vitae* [Encyclical Letter on the Regulation of Birth]. July 25, 1968. https://tinyurl.com/2p8humce.

Johnson, Elizabeth. *Creation and the Cross: The Mercy of God for a Planet in Peril.* New York: Orbis, 2018.

Joseph, Lawrence. "What Robots Can't Do and What They Shouldn't." *Commonweal* (2020).

Joy, Bill. "Why the Future Doesn't *Need* Us." *Wired.* April 2000.

Jumper, John, Kathryn Tunyasuvunakool, Pushmeet Kohli, Demis Hassabis, and the AlphaFold Team. "Computational Predictions of Protein Structures Associated with COVID-19." Research, DeepMind website. Last modified August 4, 2020. https://tinyurl.com/22hjhjjm.

Kaag, John, and Whiltel Kaufman. "Military Frameworks: Technological Know-How and the Legitimization of Warfare," *Cambridge Review of International Affairs* 22, no. 4 (December 2009): 601.

Kagan, Jerome. *What Are Emotions?* New Haven: Yale, 2007.

Kahn, Jennifer. "The Crispr Quandary." *New York Times Magazine.* November 9, 2015.

Kaku, Michio. *The Future of the Mind: The Scientific Quest to Understand, Enhance, and Empower the Mind.* New York: Anchor Books, 2015.

———. *The Future of the Mind.* New York: Doubleday, 2014.

Keller, Helen. *The Story of My Life*. New York: Grosset & Dunlap, 1905.

Kirkpatrick, Keith. "Technologizing Agriculture." *Communications of the ACM* 62, no. 2 (February 2019): 14–16, https://tinyurl.com/y6t785w9.

Kissinger, Henry. "How the Enlightenment Ends." *The Atlantic*. June 2018. https://tinyurl.com/3az35er4 (accessed August 9, 2018).

Knapton, Sarah. "AlphaGo Zero: Google DeepMind supercomputer learns 3,000 years of human knowledge in 40 days." *The Telegraph*. October 18, 2017. https://tinyurl.com/4y7ez4sx (accessed January 19, 2019).

Knight, Will. "As Workers Spread Out to Halt the Virus, Robots Fill the Gaps." *Wired*. April 4, 2020. https://tinyurl.com/54bcapbb (accessed June 7, 2020).

Kramer, Adam D. I., Jamie E. Guillory, and Jeffrey T. Hancock. "Experimental evidence of massive-scale emotional contagion through social networks." In *Proceedings of the National Academy of Sciences* 111, no. 24 (2014): 8788–90, https://tinyurl.com/2p8tvpv8.

Krishnan, Armin. *Killer Robots: Legality and Ethicality of Autonomous Weapons*. Farnham: Ashgate, 2009.

Kurzweil, Ray. *The Singularity Is Near: When Humans Transcend Biology*. New York: Penguin, 2005.

LaFrance, Adrienne. "Facebook is a Doomsday Machine." *The Atlantic*. December 15, 2020. https://tinyurl.com/3zxatd5b/ (accessed December 31, 2020).

———. "The Internet is Mostly Bots." *The Atlantic*. January 31, 2017. https://tinyurl.com/n7e2syxn (accessed February 16, 2019).

Lakoff, George, and Mark Johnson. *Philosophy in the Flesh: The Embodied Mind and Its Challenge to Western Thought*. New York: Basic Books, 1999.

Lanier, Jaron. "Agents of Alienation." *Journal of Consciousness Studies* 2, no. 3 (1995): 76–81, https://tinyurl.com/3msyffac.

———. "One Half a Manifesto." *Wired*. December 1, 2000. https://tinyurl.com/mryuw7rk.

———. "The First Church of Robotics." *New York Times*. August 9, 2010. https://tinyurl.com/bdejzpjv (accessed June 15, 2016).

———. *Ten Arguments for Deleting Your Social Media Accounts Right Now*. London: Penguin, 2018.

Laris, Michael. "Waymo Launches Nation's First Commercial Self-Driving Taxi Service in Arizona." *Washington Post*. December 5, 2018. https://tinyurl.com/53t7bnr7 (accessed June 9, 2019).

Lasch, Christopher. *The Culture of Narcissism: American Life in an Age of Diminishing Expectations*. New York: Norton, 1979.

LeCun, Yann, Yoshua Bengio, and Geoffrey Hinton. "Deep Learning." *Nature* 521, no. 28 (2015): 436–44.

Levin, Sam. "Facebook told advertisers it can identify teens feeling 'insecure' and 'worthless.'" *The Guardian*. May 1, 2017. https://tinyurl.com/3nz9cpay (accessed December 31, 2020).

Levinas, Emmanuel. *Time and the Other*. Translated by Richard Coen. Pittsburgh: Duquesne University Press, 1985.

———. *Totality and Infinity*. Pittsburgh: Duquesne University Press, 1969.

———. "Ethics as First Philosophy." In *The Levinas Reader*, translated by Sean Hand and Michael Temple, edited by Sean Hand. Oxford: Blackwell, 1989.

Libet, B., C. A. Gleason, E. W. Wright, and D. K. Pearl. "Time of conscious intention to act in relation to onset of cerebral activity (readiness-potential). The unconscious initiation of a freely voluntary act." *Brain* 106, no. 3 (1983): 623–42, https://tinyurl.com/4cps9wh4.

Lo, Felix Tun Han. "The Dilemma of Openness in Social Robots." *Techné: Research in Philosophy and Technology* 23, no. 3 (2019): 342–65, https://tinyurl.com/sa77v6vj.

Loizos, Connie. "This famous roboticist doesn't think Elon Musk understands AI." *TechCrunch*. July 19, 2017. https://tinyurl.com/2p8jpz9c (accessed September 14, 2018).

Lorrimar, Victoria. "Mind Uploading and Embodied Cognition: A Theological Response." *Zygon* 54, no. 1 (2019): 191–206.

Macfarlane, Robert. "Killing does not come easy for soldiers." *Washington Post*. October 13, 2010. https://tinyurl.com/yc3anrsz (accessed June 26, 2020).

Manyika, James, Susan Lund, Michael Chui, Jacques Bughin, Jonathan Woetzel, Parul Batra, Ryan Ko, and Saurabh Sanghvi. "What the Future of Work Will Mean for Jobs, Skills, and Wages: Jobs Lost, Jobs Gained." *McKinsey*. November 28, 2017. https://tinyurl.com/59ct2fue.

Martinez, Matthew. "'Sex robot brothel' coming to Houston, Texas, and it's legal." September 25, 2018. https://tinyurl.com/2kzdf63n (accessed June 10, 2019).

Martone, Robert. "The Neuroscience of the Gut." *Scientific American*. April 19, 2011. https://tinyurl.com/2nnebfdx.

"Masturbation." *Religious Institute*. August 7, 2009, https://tinyurl.com/598h93wv.

McFarland, Matt. "Elon Musk: 'With artificial intelligence we are summoning the demon.'" *Washington Post*. October 24, 2014. https://tinyurl.com/5n9a55vz (accessed January 20, 2020).

McLean, Stuart. "Creation and Anthropology." In *Theology Beyond Christendom: Essays on the Centenary of the Birth of Karl Barth, May 10, 1886*, edited by John Thompson, Princeton Theological Monograph Series, no. 6. Allison Park, PA: Pickwick, 1986.

Medlock, Ben. "The Body is the Missing Link for Truly Intelligent Machines." *Aeon*. https://tinyurl.com/2p92v8bs (accessed June 25, 2019).

Mehtab, Sidra, and Jaydip Sen. "A Robust Predictive Model for Stock Price Prediction Using Deep Learning and Natural Language Processing." SSRN Scholarly Paper. Rochester, NY: Social Science Research Network. December 12, 2019. https://tinyurl.com/4z5z3a2v.

Mercer, Calvin. "Whole Brain Emulation Requires Enhanced Theology, and a 'Handmaiden.'" *Theology and Science* 13, no. 2 (2015): 175–86.

Merkle, John. *Approaching God: The Way of Abraham Joshua Heschel.* Collegeville, MN: Liturgical Press, 2009.

Meyer, Robinson. "Everything We Know About Facebook's Secret Mood Manipulation Experiment." *The Atlantic*. June 28, 2014. https://tinyurl.com/yc43356n (accessed September 5, 2020).

Minsky, Marvin. *Semantic Information Processing*. Cambridge, MA: MIT Press, 1968.

Moltmann-Wendel, Elizabeth. *I Am My Body: A Theology of Embodiment*. New York: Continuum, 1994.

Moor, James. "The Dartmouth College Artificial Intelligence Conference: The Next Fifty Years," *AI Magazine*, Vol 27:4, December 15, 2006, 87, https://tinyurl.com/545zsfts.

Moravec, Hans. *Mind Children: The Future of Robot and Human Intelligence*. Cambridge, MA: Harvard University Press, 1988.

Morgenthau, Hans. *Politics among Nations*, 7th ed. New York: McGraw-Hill, 2006.

Mori, Masahiro. "The Uncanny Valley: The Original Essay by Masahiro Mori." *IEEE Spectrum*. June 12, 2012. https://tinyurl.com/4y4ak4kr (accessed January 4, 2021).

Morris, Natalie. "The race problem with Artificial Intelligence: 'Machines are learning to be racist.'" *Metro*. April 1, 2020. https://tinyurl.com/bde2wux2 (accessed June 9, 2020).

Mozur, Paul. "One Month, 500,000 Face Scans: How China Is Using AI to Profile a Minority." *New York Times*. April 14, 2019. https://tinyurl.com/2p9cs632 (accessed June 9, 2019).

Muller, Robert, III. "Report on the Investigation into Russian Interference in the 2016 Presidential Election." March 2019. https://tinyurl.com/4ankws2h.

Murphy, Kate. "Why Zoom Is Terrible." *New York Times*. April 29, 2020. https://tinyurl.com/3bpbr6tj (accessed September 6, 2020).

Murphy, Robin, Justin Adams, and Vignesh Babu Manjunath Gandudi. "How Robots Are on the Front Lines in the Battle Against COVID-19." *Smithsonian*. April 22, 2020, https://tinyurl.com/3adtuc3x.

Musk, Elon, and Brian E. Sandoval. "Elon Musk at National Governors Association 2017 Summer Meeting." National Governors Association 2017 Summer Meeting. Providence, Rhode Island. July 15, 2017, 1:04:39, https://tinyurl.com/ykejfnfa.

Nagel, Thomas. "What is it like to be a bat?" *The Philosophical Review* 83, no. 4 (1974): 435–50.

Nail, Thomas. "Artificial intelligence research may have hit a dead end." *Salon*. April 30, 2021. https://tinyurl.com/yckmw2ca (accessed May 7, 2021).

Nelson, Lisa. "The Good, the Bad, and the Ugly." *Techne: Research in Philosophy and Technology* 24, no. 1/2 (2020).

Newell, A., J. Shaw, and H. Simon. "Report on a general problem-solving program." In *Proceedings of the International Conference on Information Processing* (1959).

Niebuhr, Reinhold. "Epilogue: A View of Life from the Sidelines." In *The Essential Reinhold Niebuhr*, edited by Robert McAfee Brown. New Haven: Yale University Press, 1987.

————. *Nature and Destiny of Man*, 2 vols. New York: Scribner's, 1941–1942.

Nishimoto, Shinji, An Vu, Thomas Naselaris, Yuval Benjamini, Bin Yu, and Jack Gallant. "Reconstructing visual experiences from brain activity evoked by natural movies." *Current Biology* 21, no. 19 (2011): 1641–46, https://tinyurl.com/mr424ddr.

Nørretranders, Tor. *The User Illusion: Cutting Consciousness Down to Size*. New York: Penguin, 1991.

O'Dwyer, Rachel. "Algorithms Are Making the Same Mistakes as Humans Assessing Credit Scores." *Quartz*. May 14, 2018. https://tinyurl.com/mu8s62k3 (accessed June 9, 2019).

Ong, Walter. *Orality and Literacy: The Technologizing of the Word*. London: Routledge, 1982.

Oord, Thomas. "Can technologies promote overall well-being? Questions about love for machine-oriented societies." In *Love, Technology, and Theology*, edited by Scott Midson. London: T&T Clark, 2020.

"Our See & Spray Machines." *Blue Rivers Technology* (accessed June 9, 2020). https://tinyurl.com/26fuenmm.

Payne, Kenneth. *Strategy, Evolution, and War: From Apes to Artificial Intelligence*. Georgetown: Georgetown University Press, 2018.

Peters, Ted. "H-: Transhumanism and the Posthuman Future: Will Technological Progress Get Us There?" September 1, 2011. https://tinyurl.com/2k8kvk8f (accessed June 15, 2016).

Pinker, Steven. *How the Mind Works*. New York: W. W. Norton, 1998.

Pisani, Bob. "What Caused the Flash Crash? CFTC, DOJ Weigh In." *CNBC*. April 21, 2015. https://tinyurl.com/4mvw48s7 (accessed June 17, 2020).

Ponticus, Evagrius. *Praktikos* 1. Vol. 4, *Chapters on Prayer*. Translated by Luke Dysinger. https://tinyurl.com/yu32e26v.

"The Problem." *Campaign to Stop Killer Robots.* https://tinyurl.com/457bewbb (accessed June 26, 2020).

Rahner, Karl. *"Growing Old."* In *Prayers and Meditations: An Anthology of Spiritual Writings,* edited by J. Griffiths. New York: Crossroad, 1981.

———. "On the Theology of the Incarnation," *Theological Investigations* IV. New York: Seabury Press, 1974.

Ramakrishna, Prashanth. "'There's Just No Doubt That It Will Change the World': David Chalmers on VR and AI" *New York Times.* June 18, 2019. https://tinyurl.com/238symk8 (accessed June 25, 2019).

Rao, Rajesh, Andrea Stocco, Matthew Bryan, Devapratim Sarma, Tiffany Youngquist, Joseph Wu, and Chantel Prat. "A Direct Brain-to-Brain Interface in Humans." *PLOS One* 9, no. 11 (2014): https://tinyurl.com/29kead53.

Rasmussen, Mette. "Like a Rock or like God? The Concept of apatheia in the Monastic Theology of Evagrius of Pontus." *Studia Theologica* 59 (2005):147–62.

Regalado, Antonio. "Human-Animal Chimeras Are Gestating on US Research Farms." *MIT Technology Review.* January 6, 2016. https://tinyurl.com/m9f847je (accessed June 15, 2016).

Religious Institute. "Masturbation." August 7, 2009. https://tinyurl.com/598h93wv.

"Replacement Organs and Tissues." *Wake Forest School of Medicine.* https://tinyurl.com/yzmbjms6 (accessed June 15, 2016).

"Resolution Against Drone Warfare." *Church of the Brethren Ministry and Mission Board.* March 10, 2013. https://tinyurl.com/3as3x5d9.

Rigano, Christopher. "Using Artificial Intelligence to Address Criminal Justice Needs." National Institute of Justice. October 8, 2018. https://tinyurl.com/y7xt969x (accessed June 9, 2019).

Riley, Tonya. "Get Ready, This Year Your next Job Interview May Be with an AI Robot." *CNBC*. March 13, 2018. https://tinyurl.com/2p8nnzfy (accessed June 9, 2019).

Ritschl, Albrecht. *The Christian Doctrine of Justification and Reconciliation*. Edinburgh: T&T Clark, 1990.

Romanides, John. *The Ancestral Sin*. Ridgewood, NJ: Zephyr Publishing, 1998.

Rosenberg, Tina. "AI Joins the Campaign Against Sex Trafficking." *New York Times*. April 9, 2019. https://tinyurl.com/ywkjc5x8 (accessed June 9, 2020).

Russell, Robert John. "Jesus: The Way of all Flesh and the Proleptic Feather of Time." In Gregersen, Niels Henrick. *Incarnation: On the Scope and Depth of Christology*. Minneapolis: Fortress Press, 2015.

Šabanović, Selma, and Wan-Ling Chang. "Socializing Robots: Constructing Robotic Sociality in the Design and Use of the Assistive Robot PARO." *AI and Society* 31, no. 4 (2016): 537–51, https://tinyurl.com/2y5nvy6z.

Sacks, Oliver. "The Leg." *London Review of Books*, June 17, 1982.

Samuel, Sigal. "Robot priests can bless you, advise you, and even perform your funeral." *Vox*. January 13, 2020. https://tinyurl.com/565n275y (accessed February 11, 2021).

Scharre, Paul. *Army of None: Autonomous Weapons and the Future of War*. New York; London: W. W. Norton & Co., 2018.

Schlosser, Markus. "Agency." *Stanford Encyclopedia of Philosophy*. Last modified October 28, 2019. https://tinyurl.com/28scuc62.

Schneider, Karen. "Mission Impossible." *People Magazine*. June 1996.

Schurger, Aaron, Jacobo D. Sitt, and Stanislas Dehaene. "An Accumulator Model for Spontaneous Neural Activity Prior to Self-Initiated Movement." In *Proceedings of the National Academy of Sciences* 109, no. 42 (2012): E2904–13, https://tinyurl.com/2wvke3a3.

Schwartz, Oscar. "In 2016, Microsoft's Racist Chatbot Revealed the Dangers of Online Conversation." *IEEE Spectrum.* November 25, 2019. https://tinyurl.com/mvd5u48r (accessed September 5, 2020).

Searle, John. "Minds, Brains, and Programs." *The Behavioral and Brain Sciences* 3, no. 3 (1980): 417–24.

Shotter, John. "Listening in a Way that Recognizes/Realizes the World of the Other." *International Journal of Listening* (2009).

Shulevitz, Judith. "Alexa, How Will You Change Us?" *The Atlantic.* November 2018.

———. "Alexa, Should We Trust You?" *The Atlantic.* November 2018. https://tinyurl.com/2yr5w3fp (accessed January 5, 2021).

Sierra, Leonor. "Are we alone in the universe? Revisiting the Drake equation." *NASA Exoplanet Exploration.* May 19, 2016. https://tinyurl.com/pnx4ym79 (accessed December 24, 2018).

Silicone Soul: A Documentary by Melody Gilbert. https://tinyurl.com/mscx945w (accessed June 10, 2019).

Simon, Herbert A. "Modeling Human Mental Processes." In *Papers Presented at the May 9–11, 1961, Western Joint IRE-AIEE-ACM Computer Conference,* 111–19. IRE-AIEE-ACM '61 (Western). New York: Association for Computing Machinery, 1961. https://tinyurl.com/2p8mjrzf.

Simon, Herbert, and Allen Newell. "Computer Science as Empirical Inquiry: Symbols and Search." In *Mind Design II: Philosophy, Psychology, Artificial Intelligence,* edited by John Haugeland. Cambridge, MA: MIT, 1997.

Simon, Herbert. "Designing organizations for an information-rich world." In *Computers, Communication, and the Public Interest,* edited by Martin Greenberger. Baltimore: Johns Hopkins University Press, 1971.

———. *The Shape of Automation for Men and Management.* New York: Harper & Row, 1965.

Simon, Matt. "Your Online Shopping Habit Is Fueling a Robotics Renaissance." *Wired.* December 6, 2017. https://tinyurl .com/2p859yrb (accessed June 9, 2019).

Simonite, Tom. "How Google Plans to Solve Artificial Intelligence." *MIT Technology Review.* March 31, 2016, https://tinyurl .com/3wr65ych.

————. "Moore's Law is Dead. Now What?" *MIT Technology Review.* May 13, 2016. https://tinyurl.com/4h53dts6.

Sittler, Joseph. "A Theology for Earth." *The Christian Scholar* 37 (1954): 371–72.

Slayton, Rebecca. "The Promise and Peril of Artificial Intelligence: A Brief History." *War on the Rocks.* June 8, 2020. https://tinyurl .com/yckvdfxh (accessed Jun 26, 2020).

Snape, Adam. "Over Three Quarters of Brits Say Their Social Media Page Is a Lie." *The Custard Blog* (blog). *Custard Online Marketing Ltd.* April 6, 2016. https://tinyurl.com/jw2h29jd.

"Sophia." *Hanson Robotics.* https://tinyurl.com/ykbsv8fv (accessed June 7, 2019).

Sparrow, Robert. "Killer Robots." *Journal of Applied Philosophy* 24, no. 1 (2007): https://tinyurl.com/yc5a4s4b.

Sparrow, Robert, and Linda Sparrow. "In the Hands of Machines? The Future of Aged Care." *Minds and Machines* 16, no. 2 (2006): 141–61, https://tinyurl.com/yckave8j.

Steinberg, Michael. *A New Biology of Religion: Spiritual Practice and the Life of the Body.* Santa Barbara: Praeger, 2012.

Steiner, Peter. "On the internet, nobody knows you're a dog," illustration. *The New Yorker.* July 5, 1993. https://tinyurl.com/2p9fnmny.

Stoltzfus, Michael. "Sexual Intimacy, Spiritual Belonging, and Christian Theology." *Journal of Lutheran Ethics* 4, no. 6 (June 2004): https://tinyurl.com/yckhpjp6.

Telford, Taylor. "'Emotion detection' AI is a $20 billion industry. New research says it can't do what it claims." *Washington Post*. July 31, 2019. https://tinyurl.com/4ez35n64 (accessed August 7, 2019).

Thomas, M. E. "Confessions of a Sociopath." *Psychology Today* 43, no. 3, (2013): 52–61.

Thomas, Mike. "The Future of Artificial Intelligence." *Built In*. June 8, 2019. https://tinyurl.com/4kcdyrvc (accessed June 19, 2021).

Tirosh-Samuelson, Hava. "Engaging Transhumanism," in *H+: Transhumanism and its Critics*, ed. Gregory Hansell and William Grassie. San Francisco: Metanexus, 2011.

Turkle, Sherry. *Alone Together: Why We Expect More from Technology and Less from Each Other*. New York: Basic Books, 2011.

Twenge, Jean. *iGen: Why Today's Super-Connected Kids are Growing up Less Rebellious, More Tolerant, Less Happy, and Completely Unprepared for Adulthood*. New York: Atria, 2017.

Twitter. "HitchBOT (@hitchBOT)." https://tinyurl.com/59e6vvxm (accessed March 22, 2022).

US Department of Defense. "Summary of the 2018 Department of Defense Artificial Intelligence Strategy: Harnessing AI to Advance Our Security and Prosperity." 2018. https://tinyurl.com/yc78zk4v (accessed June 18, 2020).

Vailshery, Lionel Sujay. "Installed base of smart speakers worldwide in 2020 and 2024." *Statista*. https://tinyurl.com/2p92es5d.

van Creveld, Martin. "War and Technology." *Foreign Policy Institute*. October 24, 2007. https://tinyurl.com/bdesxuwd (accessed January 14, 2019).

Vincent, James. "DeepMind's AI Can Detect over 50 Eye Diseases as Accurately as a Doctor." *The Verge*. August 13, 2018. https://tinyurl.com/22nzyta8 (accessed June 9, 2019).

Walzer, Michael. *Just and Unjust Wars: A Moral Argument with Historical Illustrations*. New York: Basic Books, 1977.

Weil, Simone. *Waiting on God*. Translated by Emma Crawford. New York: G. P. Putnam's Sons, 1951.

Weizenbaum, Joseph. *Computer Power and Human Reason: From Judgment to Calculation*. New York: W. H. Freeman, 1976.

Wiener, Norbert. *The Human Use of Human Beings*. Boston: Houghton Mifflin, 1954.

Wildman, Wesley. "An Introduction to Relational Ontology." (2009). https://tinyurl.com/2p82ecjp.

Winograd, Terry, and Fernando Flores. *Understanding Computers and Cognition: a New Foundation for Design*. Norwood, NJ: Ablex, 1986; Reading, MA: Addison-Wesley, 1991.

Wittgenstein, Ludwig. *Tractatus Logico-Philosophicus*. London: Routledge & Kegan Paul, 1960.

Wong, Julia Carrie. "Neuralink: Elon Musk unveils pig he claims has computer implant in brain." *The Guardian*. August 28, 2020.

World Transhuman Association. "Artificial Intelligence and Transhumanism." https://tinyurl.com/yjvpc6h3 (accessed July 11, 2016).

Yapching, Mark. "Fear of death is the reason behind religious faith—Larry King." *Christianity Today*. February 28, 2015. https://tinyurl.com/4jsataft.

Zuboff, Shoshana. "You Are Now Remotely Controlled." *New York Times*. January 24, 2020. https://tinyurl.com/2p8e69d2.

Index